ɪa

The Kabbalah of the Ari Z'al,
according to the Ramhal
Rabbi Moshe Hayim Luzzatto

כללות האילן הקדוש

Translated and commented by Rabbi Raphaël Afilalo

The notes and commentaries are based on the works of the
Ramhal and particularly on:

קלח פתחי חכמה & פתחי חכמה ודעת

From the same author:
La Kabbalah du Ari Z'al, selon le Ramhal

www.ravraphael.com
ravraphael@yahoo.com

Kabbalah Editions
Montreal 2004

ISBN 2-923241-01-0

Publisher's Cataloging-in-Publication

Afilalo, Raphael
  The Kabbalah of the Ari Z'al: according to the Ramhal
p.cm.
Includes bibliographical references and index.
ISBN 2-923241-01-0 (hard cover)
1.Cabala. 2. Mysticism—Judaism. I. Afilalo, Raphael. II.
Title.
BM525. BM723 2005
296.1'6   2005909207

To Armand and Ria Afilalo

Approbation

To the attention of Rabbi Raphael Afilalo

I have well looked into this grand and important work that you have accomplished, by translating and explaining the book "Klalout Hailan", by the man of G-od; Rabbi Moshe Hayim Luzzatto.

What a benefaction of something done in its proper time; when at present the obscurity is growing and many publications deform the true wisdom (Kabbalah) with obscure mystical texts.

Now, a great man has arrived, and done reparation with his exact translation and explanation of this science.

I have read through this text, and found a work well done and with great exactitude, worth being published in this period of end of times.

With all the blessings of the Torah,

Rav Mordekhai Chriqui

בית כנסת • כולל אברכים • כולל ערב • מכון הוצאה לאור • קרן הבנין

ת.ד. 43204 רח' קטנלבוגן 73 ירושלים 91400 • טל: 02-6535101 Tel • פקס: 02-6510821 Fax • Israel ,91400 Jerusalem ,73 Katenelbogen ,43204 .B.P

ב"ה

MORDECHAI ELIAHU
FORMER CHIEF RABBI OF ISRAEL & RICHON LEZION

מרדכי אליהו
הראשון לציון והרב הראשי לישראל לשעבר

APPROBATION

ב"ה

יג' שבט תש"ס

ראה ראיתי מה שפתח הרב
המפורס' ר' מרדכי שליט"א
הסבא קמא הרב'
הראשון ...
...

GRAND RABBINAT DU QUÉBEC

To Rav Raphael Afilalo

Dear Raphael,

It is with great pleasure that I have read your book, which brings to the public the explanation of the themes of the Lurianic Kabbalah, as seen by our master the Ramhal.

It is obvious that your efforts invested in this work, will lead to the results that your translation and commentaries will be of a great contribution to those who seek to study Kabbalah.

With the blessings of the Torah,

Dr. David Sabbah, Grand Rabbin

Rabbi David R. Banon
4773 Rue Clemenceau
Chomedey- Laval
P.Q H7w 2j5
Tel: (450)-681-5412
Fax: (514)-341-0594

דוד רפאל באנון
רומ"ץ ק"ק ספרדית בלאוואל
וחבד"ץ דמונטריאל יע"א

הסכמה

בס"ד לפני ידידי הרב רפאל לבללו שי' הזי כאחנו
הק׳ שמואריאל זהו ויזדו ספר חשוב "קלת הורי זל אל ב
הראהל לכי ואשר יצא ולרה כדי להגיל את שמון
הקבלה לדוזרי השות לרבת ואשלו כדי להגיל
אל ליאוג הקבלה של שלחנם ועל ידי הק׳ תפלה
לדוך שישוין לחבר עוז כהנא וכהנה וכבות הראהל
ואמון לו ולדרריו אתריו סלו/.

החתם לכ׳ התירה היום חל אה אדר תשם

דוד רפאל באנון
הק׳ ? שמואל ריאל

Table of contents

The study of Kabbalah

There are in the Torah two commandments, among all the positive commandments, which indicate to us, how to serve our Creator:

"וידעת היום והשבת אל-לבבך כי יהוה הוא האלהים בשמים ממעל
ועל-הארץ מתחת אין עוד"

"Know therefore this day, and consider it in your heart, that the Lord is G-d in heaven above, and upon the earth beneath; there is no other." (Devarim. 4-39)

"ושמרת את-חקיו ואת-מצותיו אשר אנכי מצוך היום אשר ייטב לך
ולבניך אחריך ולמען תאריך ימים על-האדמה אשר יהוה אלהיך נתן
לך כל-הימים"

"You shall keep his statutes, and his commandments, which I command you this day, that it may go well with you, and with your children after you, and that you may prolong your days upon the land, which the Lord your G-d gives you forever." (Devarim. 4-40)

The first, clearly instructs us to know our Creator, the second, to respect and accomplish the commandments of the Torah.

These two commandments follow each other, at first, is the knowledge of the uniqueness and the will of G-d, "in heaven above"; namely in what is not visible to us, as the upper worlds and the forces[1] that execute His will, and "upon the earth beneath"; namely in the manifestations of His will, and the effects of our actions. And in second, the observance and accomplishment of the commandments. They follow each other as to affirm, that it is only after the comprehension of His will, that we are truly able to observe and accomplish His laws and commandments.

All the Kabbalists agree to say that it is not possible to understand, or to have the slightest notion of His Nature, since our comprehension cannot attain that level. However, we can learn to understand His will, how and why He created the world, in what way He directs it, the provenance of the souls and angels, the purpose of the existence of evil, the reasons for the dualism of reward and punishment, etc.

The Kabbalah is the only science that, in the least details, explains to us the true guidance of the world, so that we may understand His will.

The Kabbalah also teaches us that the world is guided by an extremely complex system of forces or lights, which through their interactions, provoke chain reactions that impact directly on man and the worlds. Each one of these reactions has numerous ramifications, with many details and results. The Kabbalah also demonstrates to us the importance of man, because only he, by getting closer to the Creator, can influence these incredible forces.

---

[1] Lights - *Sephirot*

The Torah contains four levels of comprehension, of which the highest is the *Sod*[2]. At this level, we understand that our *Tefilot* and the accomplishment of each one of the *Mitsvot,* has a direct influence on the superior worlds and on their guidance. Therefore, we see that a true understanding of the will of the Creator is possible only through the knowledge of Kabbalah, which teaches us the profound secrets of our holy Torah.

The word Kabbalah comes from the verb *Lekabel* (to receive), but to receive it is first necessary to want, and to be a *Keli*[3] able to receive and contain this knowledge. When man decides that he wants to know his Creator, in learning this science he realizes his smallness compared to these incredible forces, the perfection of the Lord and His infinite love for His creatures.

It is only by learning Kabbalah that we can accomplish the commandment of "וידעת היום" - "Know therefore this day", and understand what we are allowed to know of G-d: His will, how He guides the world, and how we can participate and influence this guidance. As it is written:

"ובקשתם משם את־יהוה אלהיך ומצאת כי תדרשנו בכל־לבבך
ובכל־נפשך"

"From there, you shall seek the Lord your G-d, and you shall find him, if you seek him with all your heart, and with all your soul." (Devarim 4-29)

---

[2] Secret
[3] Vessel, recipient

The life of the Ramhal

Ramhal are the initials of Rabbi Moshe Haim Luzzatto, who was born in the Ghetto of Padua in Italy in 1707. Son of Jacob Vita and Diamente Luzzatto, noble but modest and pious parents. Ramhal was placed in the Yeshiva, while other parents preferred the faculty of Medicine of the University of Padua. From an early age, he showed an exceptional talent for the study of Kabbalah, in a letter sent by his friend and student Rav Yekoutiel Gordon to Rabbi Mordekhai Yaffe of Vilna, we read:

> "Ramhal was only fourteen, yet he already knew all the Kabbalah of the Ari Z'al by heart, and nobody knew about it, not even his parents."

At the age of fifteen, he already had written his first book[4] of Kabbalah. His Rav and teacher; Rabbi Isaiah Bassan, a well known Talmud scholar, and one of the most important Rabbis of Italy, wrote:

> "I have communicated to him all the steps of the knowledge, and all my spiritual possessions were at his disposition; nothing was hidden to this genius thirsty for knowledge. He was searching my entire library to find some of the writings of Kabbalah that G-d had granted me, then he would cross the stream, tasting the "Etz Hayim". His mind would then enter

---

[4] Prof. Meir Benayahou, "Kabbalistic writings of R. M. H. Luzzatto."

the valleys of secrets, and began to love and delight in them...[5]"

At the age of seventeen, Ramhal denotes certain contradictions in the "Etz Hayim"[6], and composed his book "*Leshone Limoudim*", in which he stated the modern rules of gender, stylistics, rhetoric and versification, as a guide to the Hebrew writer. Ramhal demonstrated particular abilities in using metaphors and assonances, and he used this ability with great efficiency in his different dramatic writings. For this, Ramhal would be proclaimed "the father of modern Hebrew literature"[7].

Later, a *Maggid*[8] revealed himself to the Ramhal. In a letter to Rav Benjamin Hacohen in December 1729, he wrote:

"While I was meditating on a *Yihud*[9] I fell asleep, and when I woke up, I heard a voice saying: "I have come down to reveal hidden secrets of the Holy King." I remained trembling for a moment, then took hold of myself, ... the voice did not stop revealing mysterious things. The day after, at the same time, I took the precaution of being alone in my room, the voice manifested itself to reveal another secret, until the day that it revealed to me that it was a *Maggid* .... Three

---

[5] Iguerot (correspondance) p. 59
[6] Iguerot p. 5
[7] Rav Mordekhai Chriqui; "Rabbi Moshe Hayim Luzzatto, Le flambeau de la Cabale"
[8] Celestial Mentor
[9] Unification

months later, he transmitted to me other *Yihudim* to do everyday, in order to merit the visit of Eliyahu Hanavi [10] .... Then Eliyahu Hanavi came to reveal celestial secrets, and he later announced the coming of *Mettat'ron* – The great Prince of the angels...."

Under the dictation of the *Maggid*, Ramhal wrote thousands of pages and revealed magnificent secrets.

A mystical study group was formed around the Ramhal, its goal: the *Tikun* of the *Shekhina* and of all *Israel,* and the continual reading of the *Zohar*[11]. The adherence to this group required conforming to the rules of purity and devotions written, and signed by the members.

Once the goals of this study group and the revelation of the *Maggid* became known, some Rabbis, and particularly the Rav Moshe Haggiz, started to make war against the Ramhal. For them, because of the rift created within the Jewish community by the pseudo-messianic movement of Shabbetai Tsevi [12], mysticism and Kabbalah were synonymous with threats, and endangerment for the community.

This war, or rather persecution, since the attacks were coming only from one side, is largely described in the correspondence between Ramhal and his Rav; Rabbi Bassan [13]. One letter

---

[10] The prophet Elijah

[11] This continual reading of the *Zohar* has been re-instated today at Beth Ramhal in Jerusalem by Rav Mordekhai Chriqui.

[12] False Messiah who converted to Islam in 1666

[13] Largely reported and commented by Rav Mordekhai Chriqui, in "Rabbi Moshe Hayim Luzzatto, le flambeau de la Cabale"

written by the Ramhal to Rav Bassan clearly demonstrates his peaceful spirit, being above such petty quarrels:

> "Try by your wisdom, master, to refute their arguments ... For what purpose this quarrel ... I do not want to create conflicts with anybody ... It is peace that we need ..."

To Rabbi Moshe Haggiz Ramhal wrote:

> "To the illustrious wise ... his name is among the greats... son of righteous ... how come you, a sage – like an angel of G-d, have gone to war without trying to delve into the problem; to declare war against someone you have never met or seen ... No, it is not a good thing. In any case, let us stop this quarrel ... let us not give to the Satan room to dance between us..."

For five years, the period of persecution is extended, we see Ramhal trying to defend himself and respond to accusations, particularly those of the Rabbinical Court of Hamburg, whose chief was Rabbi Ezekiel Katzenellenbogen[14]. Yet, what was he really blamed for? Nothing specifically, except perhaps to have written on the subject of Kabbalah, to have mentioned the Messiah, and to have revealed his communications with the *Maggid*. Yet never, and in none of his writings, did the

---

[14] "By coincidence" the unique center dedicated to the Ramhal, Beth Ramhal created by Rav Mordekhai Chriqui, is situated on Katzenellenbogen Street, in Jerusalem

Ramhal allude to himself as the Messiah, or any type of savior. In one of his letters to the Rabbis of Livourne, he wrote:

> "Miracles I do not do, to predict the future also not. In reality, many people gather around me to study Torah. Afterwards, I write books, as permitted by the Lord ... Even the magicians of Pharaoh made miracles in front of Moses ... And to my humble opinion, it is not the right way to verify the contents of a wisdom."

Despite this very clear declaration, and on the insistence of the Rabbi M. Haggiz, Ramhal agrees in 1730 to sign a document stating that he officially retracted his writings, and agreed that:

> "The duty of every Jew is to obey the orders of the Rabbis, even if they say that the right hand is the left, and the left hand is the right, and to stop writing in the language of the *Zohar* on Kabbalah, in the name of the *Maggid* or other holy Souls; so as not to provoke quarrels in the midst of the wise of Israel"

Following this undertaking, Ramhal sent all his Kabbalistic writings prior to 1730 to Rabbi Bassan, who sealed them in a case and forwarded them to Rabbi Moshe Alprun in Padoua.

From 1730 to 1734, Ramhal wrote more than 40 works on Kabbalah, but not in the name of the *Maggid*, out of respect for his agreement, but rather in a subtle and rational language.

In 1735 at the age of 28, and after years of harassment, he left Italy and settled in Holland.

Passing by Frankfurt, Ramhal encountered the Dayan Rabbi Ya'acov Papiroch, who commended him to leave, and forced him to sign another agreement preventing him from writing on Kabbalah or studying its works with anyone. Nevertheless, he retained the right to study the works of the Ari Z'al from the age of 40, which unfortunately he never reached[15].

It was only in 1736, following the death of his teacher Rabbi Bassan, the serious illness of Rabbi Haggiz and the burial of the trunk containing the manuscripts, that things began to calm.

In Amsterdam, a period of relative tranquility lasted until 1743, there, Ramhal is appointed Rosh Yeshiva and writes his best-known book, and one of the most studied in *Yeshivot* to this day: *Messilat Yesharim* (The Path of the Just[16]), a masterpiece of ethics, not moralizing. He also published two other important works: *Da'at Tevunot* (The Knowing Heart[17]), and *Derech Hashem* (The Way of G-d[18]).

In 1743, Ramhal fulfilled his dream of settling in Eretz Israel, for as our sages say: "Living in Eretz Israel, is a commandment encompassing all of the Torah."[19] Very few details are known about his life there, except that he lived in the city of Akko, near Tiberias. Yet his stay in Israel lasted

---

[15] Like the Ari Z'al, who died before the age of forty
[16] Translated into English by Rav Shraga Silverstein, Philipp Feildheim, Publisher
[17] Translated into English by Rav Shraga Silverstein, Philipp Feildheim, Publisher
[18] Translated into English by Rav Shraga Silverstein, Philipp Feildheim, Publisher
[19] Or Ha'haim (Devarim, 30, 20)

only a short period, as he died along with his family during a plague in 1746, at the age of 39.

One question raised, is whether Ramhal wrote any books in Eretz Israel. None are known to date, but it is hard to believe that after being persecuted for his Kabbalistic writings, that he would have refrained from doing so, now that he had finaly found his freedom.

Like many great geniuses, Ramhal was recognized as such only after his death. The Gaon of Vilna declared that if Ramhal was still alive, he would have traveled to Italy on foot to learn from his wisdom. About Messilat Yesharim, he said:

> "This book is witness to the greatness of its author, and his extraordinary vision of the human potential for elevation..."

The *Maggid* of Mezritch said:

> "His generation did not merit this great man.... Many among our people, through lack of knowledge, have uttered on this saintly man calumny that was not justified."

It is a pity that some Rabbis of his generation mistook him as an impostor, and prevented him from bequeathing to the people of Israel other magnificent works.

We should pray for our generation to merit the revealing of all his writings, and particularly of the *"Zohar Tiniana"*[20], which was buried along with his other writings, by the Rabbis of Frankfurt. Amen.

---

[20] The second Zohar

Introduction

The translation and explanation of this book have two objectives: the first, is to make the Ramhal better known to the English-speaking public, the second, is to provide a genuine picture of the true Kabbalah. Unfortunately, there are today an enormous number of books that use the name "Kabbalah" in their title, yet the great majority does not deal with Kabbalah at all, but rather of often questionable esoteric subjects.

The book of the Ramhal "כללות האילן הקדוש" or "The Essentials of the Tree of Life" is a summary of the master work of the Ari Z'al ; "The Etz Hayim" (The Tree of Life). It describes the evolution of the worlds, the *Sephirot* and the *Partsufim*, in a clear and concise language, which only retains the essential. Divided into ten chapters, it starts with the first manifestation of the creation, the superior worlds, the *Sephirot*, until explaining to us the systems of reincarnation of the souls.

The Ramhal explains, that in order to learn the wisdom of Kabbalah, which is profuse with details, it is first necessary to have an image, or a general idea of the *Sephirotic* tree. Once familiar with this general idea, we can start to study and understand all the details that will further clarify this first image.

It is also necessary to be familiar with the terms and appellations used, because in the language of Kabbalah, anthropomorphisms are used only to illustrate the esoteric power of these forces. It is well understood, that there is no physical existence at these higher levels. Thus, when terms such as mouth, ears, or other body parts are used, the intention is to describe the metaphor, or the position they symbolize.

The journey to understand the wisdom of Kabbalah is a long one, yet one that is very gratifying. As in every journey, it is necessary to take a first step. A thorough study of this book, along with other books of the Ramhal, will allow the reader to advance in a slow but steady pace towards an understanding of what Kabbalah truly is.

I would like to thank my wife Simona for her patience and encouragement. I would also like to thank a true friend, Rav Mordekhai Chriqui (who first introduced me to Kabbalah) for his important input to this book. May G-d help him to continue spreading the knowledge of the Ramhal and his writings throughout the world. Finally, I am very grateful to a special person, my brother Armand, for his friendship and constant support. May G-d bestow on him His blessings, and grant him health, success and happiness.

Note

The original book "כללות האילן הקדוש" *or "The Essentials of the Tree of Life" is a short book of about 17 pages. Facing the Hebrew text (also in grey) is the translation. Below the grey, I have tried to explain and comment this obscure and concentrated text. I have, when necessary, added notes in brackets or at the bottom of the page.*

First chapter

The Uniqueness, the *Tsimtsum,*
Adam Kadmon

Introduction

In the beginning, there was no existence except His presence. His light or energy being of such intensity, no existence in His proximity was possible. His first act in this creation was to contract His light from a certain space, so as to reduce its intensity, and allow created beings to exist. After this contraction, a ray of His light entered this empty space, and formed the first Sephirot. A first world; "Adam Kadmon" was created, from it; came out other lights - Sephirot. These Sephirot, which did not have individual receptacles, went back up to their source, and came out differently. This is called 'Olam Ha'Akudim (the world of the attached).

a) Until the world was created, He and His Name were One.
He willed [to create], and contracted His light to create all beings, by giving them a space. There is no existence that does not have its space.

The space [from where the light contracted] being circular, the *Ein Sof* [21] encircles it from all sides.
A ray [*Kav*] emerged from Him, entered on one side, and made all the levels[22].

א. עד שלא נברא העולם היה
הוא ושמו אחד.
רצה וצמצם אורו לברוא כל
הבריות, נתן להם מקום.
אין לך דבר שאין לו מקום.

נמצא המקום שווה לכולם.
והאין סוף ב"ה מקיפו לכל צד.
וקו יוצא ממנו לצד אחד,
בוקע ונכנס, ועושה כל
המדרגות.

At first, the Creator was alone, occupying all space with His light [23]. His light without end, borders or limit, filled everything. He was not bestowing his influence, because there was no one to receive it. When He willed to create, He started to influence. His light being of such holiness and intensity, it is not possible for any being to exist in its proximity. His first act in this creation, was then to set limits to His light, so that it would not emanate with its full force.

---

[21] The infinite, literally, "without end"
[22] *Sephirot*
[23] Emanation, presence

By these boundaries, He revealed the concepts of rigor and limit, needed by the created beings, and gave a space for all the created to exist. This is called the *"Tsimtsum"*[24] of the *Ein Sof;* the retraction of His light from a certain space, and encircling it. This round space is called *"Hallal"*[25], and contains all possibilities of existence for separated entities, given that they are distanced from the intensity of His light.

When His light retracted, forming the round space, a trace of it, called the *Reshimu*[26], remained inside. This lower intensity light, allowed a space of existence (*Makom*), for all the created worlds and beings. By "space", one should not understand a physical space, but rather a possibility of existence. The roots of all future existence and events are in the *"Reshimu"*. Nothing can come into existence, without having its root in this imprint. However, only the Emanator decides what comes to existence, since He guides all.

From the *Ein Sof*, a straight ray of light called *"Kav"*[27], entered the *Hallal*. The combination of the *Kav* and the *Reshimu* is what will give existence to the *Sephirot* with which He governs the worlds. What the *Kav* is to the *Reshimu,* the soul is to the body.

---

[24] Retraction of His light
[25] Empty space, vacuum
[26] Imprint - trace
[27] Ray

They [The *Sephirot*] are ten levels, with incommensurable qualities. Ten encircling, and in their middle, ten linear, which have the qualities of the *Ein Sof:* kindness, rigor and mercy.

עשר מדרגות הן, מדתן שאין
להם סוף.
עשרה עגולים, ויושרם
באמצעם,
שבהם מידותיו של מקום –
חסד, דין, רחמים.

He directs His creatures with justice, rewarding and punishing, returning all evil to goodness, and bringing all His creatures to His will. As it is written:
" I am first and I am last, and beside Me there is no G-d." (Isaiah, 44, 6).

מנהג כל בריותיו במשפט,
משכיר ומעניש,
ומחזיר כל רעה לטובה,
ומביא בריותיו לרצונו.
וכן הוא אומר (ישעיה מד, י) :
"אני ראשון ואני אחרון
ומבלעדי אין אלהים". (כז-כח)

All that G-d created in His world, He created only for His glory, as it is said:
"All that is called by My Name and glory, I created, formed and even made."
(Isaiah, 43, 7).
And He said: "G-d will reign for ever." (Shemot, 15, 18)

כל מה שברא הקב"ה בעולמו
לא בראו אלא לכבודו,
שנאמר (ישעיה מג, ז) :
"כל הנקרא בשמי ולכבודי
בראתיו יצרתיו אף עשיתיו".

ואומר (שמות טו, יח) :
"ה' ימלוך לעולם ועד" .

After entering the Hallal, the *Kav* made ten circles encircling one another, but still maintaining a straight shape[28]. These ten circles are called *Sephirot Ha'igulim* (encircling *Sephirot*). They are in charge of the general guidance of the worlds, and are not influenced by the actions of men.

From the *Kav,* another ten *Sephirot* were formed, but this time in a linear arrangement, and later in three columns: right, left and middle, representing the guidance of the world in the manner of *'Hesed, Din* and *Rahamim* (Kindness, rigor and mercy). This guidance is dependent on time, and the actions of men.

b) Ten *Sephirot,* internal and external; their shape, as of a man[29], the first of them; *Adam Kadmon* (Primordial Man). From the lights that were invested inside of him, came out [ramifications] his four senses: sight, hearing, smell and speech.	ב. עשר ספירות פנימיות וחיצוניות דמיונן כמראה אדם. הראשון שבכולם - אדם קדמון. וממה שנגבל בפנים יוצאים ארבע חושים חלק ממנו : רש"ר"ד. (כט)

The *Sephirot* are the qualities or particularities of forces, by which the *Ein Sof* directs the worlds. His light is perfect, and cannot be measured by any definition or limiting terms. If we think about definitions, we introduce a notion of limit, or absence of its opposite. However, the concept of limitlessness is beyond our human comprehension, and we therefore have to

---

[28] The *Kav*

[29] The shape of the *Sephirotic* tree resembles the shape of man

use terms accessible to our understanding. Being ourselves distinct separate beings, we cannot grasp the concept of the "non-distinct", everything we know is finite, by having a measure or an opposite. The term 'quality' is used here only to help us understand the effect of His light upon the guidance of the worlds.

Each *Sephira* is composed of a vessel called *Keli*[30], which holds its part of light called *Or*[31]. There are many details to this union of *Or* and *Keli,* as we will see further on. There is no difference in the *Or* itself; the difference comes from the particularity, or position of the *Sephira*. When we think about the guidance of the world, we see it directed by kindness, rigor or mercy, and this, in different measures, or mixtures. Since the *Sephirot* are the links between the Emanator and the guidance of the world, we now understand their division into these three qualities.

---

[30] Vessel, receptacle or vase
[31] Light, energy or force

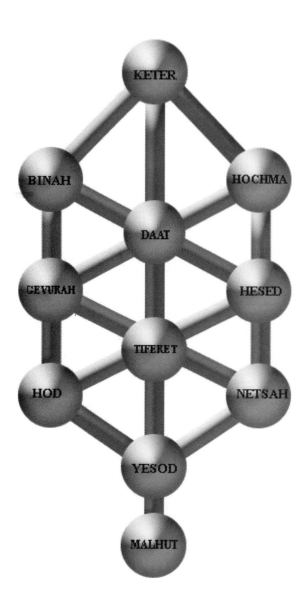

There are ten *Sephirot*, their names are: *Keter, 'Hokhma, Binah, 'Hesed, Gevurah, Tiferet, Netsah, Hod, Yesod, Mal'hut.*

On the right, the *'Hesed* (kindness) column: *'Hokhma, 'Hesed, Netsah.*
In the Middle, the *Rahamim* (mercy) column: *Keter, Tiferet, Yesod, Mal'hut*
On the left, the *Din* (rigor) column: *Binah, Gevurah, Hod.*
There is one more *Sephira* called *Da'at*, which is counted when *Keter* is not, also in the *Rahamim* column.

Since the intention of the Creator is to bestow goodness on His creatures, all the levels of creation were put in place so His kindness could emanate to them, yet in such a way that they would be able to receive it. The first configuration, by which the emanated light was formed into ten *Sephirot*, is called *Adam Kadmon* (Primordial Man). It is the union between the *Reshimu* and the *Kav*, and from this first configuration, all the worlds came forth into existence.

The *Reshimu* is the exteriority, the *Kav* the interiority. *Adam Kadmon* being at such close proximity to the *Ein Sof*, we cannot grasp anything of its nature. Our understanding only starts from what came out of him, in the way of his senses; which are called his branches.

From *Adam Kadmon* emerged numerous worlds, four of which are called: sight, hearing, smell and speech; that spread out from his eyes, ears, nose, and mouth. In the language of Kabbalah, we use names of body parts solely to illustrate the esoteric powers of these forces. It is understood, of course, that there is no physical existence at these level. When we say ears, mouth, or any other physical expression, the goal is to describe the inner sense, or the position they represent.

These emanations are in the order of the name יקוק. All the configurations are drawn from the four letters of the Name of H. *B'H*, and their different spellings, which are called *Miluim*[32].

The four names are *'AV*, *SaG*, *MaH*, *BaN*. (ע"ב, ס"ג, מ"ה, ב'ן)

c) From the four letters of הוי"ה ב"ה, there are Four Miluim: ע"ב, ס"ג, מ"ה, ב'ן - ('AV, SaG, MaH, BaN)	ג. ד' אותיות הוי"ה ב"ה
- *Ta'amim* [cantillation notes]	ד' מלואים: עסמ"ב
- *Nekudot* [vowels]	ע"ב, ס"ג, מ"ה, ב'ן
- *Tagin* [crowns]	טנת"א
- *Autiot* [letters] They include one, in the other[33].	טעמים. נקודות תגין אותיות נכללים אלו מאלו
ע"ב ('AV) is in the head, its ramifications are mysterious; they come out from the hair on the head.	ע"ב בגולגולת, ענפיו נעלמים, מן השערות של הראש הם יוצאים.

---

[32] Spelling of each letter separately

[33] The *Ta'amim* corresponds to the name of *'AV*, the *Nekoudot* to the name of *SaG*, *the Tagin* to *MaH* and the *Autiot* to *BaN*. The *Ta'amim* also have an aspect of *SaG* (*SaG* of *'AV*) and so on

[34] The *Sephirot*

ס"ג (*SaG*) came out from the ears and downward. Its cantillation notes subdivide in three levels: higher, middle and lower. The higher [are] from the ears, the middle from the nose, and the lower from the mouth.

The higher came out from the ears, ten [*Sephirot*] from the right, and ten from the left, these internal, and these encircling. They all include in one ה, which is shaped as ו ד. How far do they descend? Until the end of the beard on the chin.

The middle, came out from the nose, ten [*Sephirot*] from the right, and ten from the left, these internal, and these encircling. They approached [34] each other, and then the ו of the ה was revealed, with six *Alephs* [א א א א א א], coming out and downward, reaching to the chest.

יצא ס״ג מן האזנים ולמטה.
טעמים שלו ג׳ מינים :
עליונים, תחתונים, אמצעים.
עליונים באזנים,
אמצעים בחוטם,
תחתונים בפה

יצאו עליונים מן האזנים,
עשרה מהימין ועשרה מהשמאל,
אלו פנימים ואלו מקיפים לגביהם,
כלולים בה׳ אחת שצורתה ד"ו.
עד היכן הם יורדין ?
עד כנגד שבולת הזקן.

יצאו אמצעים מן החוטם,
עשרה מימין, ועשרה משמאל,
אלו פנימים, ואלו מקיפים
לגביהם.
והרי נתקרבו זה לגבי זה,
ונתגלתה ו׳ של ה׳ בששה אלפין.
יוצאים ויורדין עד החזה.

Depending on the *Miluim* (spelling) of the letters, we obtain different names as:

יוד הי ויו הי - עב	- *'AV* = 72
יוד הי ואו הי - סג	- *SaG* = 63
יוד הא ואו הא - מה	- *MaH* = 45
יוד הה וו הה - בן	- *BaN* = 52

Each name can also be subdivided as:
'AV of *'AV*, *SaG* of *'AV*, *MaH* of *'AV* ...*BaN* of *BaN* etc.

The reading of the Torah is incomplete without the *Ta'amim*, *Nekudot*, *Tagin*, and *Autiot*. The *Ta'amim* (cantillation marks) are of the highest level and are subdivided in three: higher, middle and lower. The *Nekudot* (vowels) are second, also in three levels: higher, middle and lower. The *Tagin* (crowns) are third, and appear on top of some letters only. The *Autiot* (letters) are fourth. When reading in a Sepher Torah, one sees the *Autiot* and the *Tagin*, has to guess logically the vowels, and learn by tradition the *Ta'amim*.

The "branches" are the lights that spread forth from *Adam Kadmon*, by way of its apertures in the head. The first one to come out is the branch of *'AV*, which spread out from the hair on its head. This light is too lofty for our understanding.

From *'AV* of *SaG*, came out three branches in the aspects of the *Ta'amim*: higher, middle and lower. They came out through the ears, nose, and mouth: the higher from the ears, the middle from the nose, and the lower from the mouth.

From the ears came out ten linear *Sephirot* from the left ear, and ten encircling *Sephirot* from the right ear, they went down until the beard on the chin. From the nose, came out ten encircling *Sephirot* from the right nostril, and ten linear from the left nostril, they went down until the chest, closer together than the lights from the ears, but still separated. The lights of the encircling *Sephirot* are of a finer aspect, which is why they came out of the right side; the side of *'Hesed* [kindness], as opposed to the left; which is of the side of *Gevurah* [rigor]. In the emanations [lights] of the ears and nose, there is not yet a concept of *Keli* [vessel].

The lower [*Ta'amim*] came out from the mouth, ten internal [*Sephirot*], and ten encircling [*Sephirot*], in this way was revealed the ד of the ה, with four Aleph [א א א א], two יי, and two יוד.	יצאו התחתונים מן הפה, י׳ פנימים וי׳ מקיפים, ונתגלתה הד׳ שבה׳ בד׳ אלפין, שנים יו׳, ושנים יוד.
From the two ears and the two nostrils; two vapors from the right side of the mouth, and two utterances from the left side, they are rooted in the two jaws, upper and lower. They come out, and descend until the navel.	מב׳ אזנים ומב׳ נחירים — ב׳ הבלים בימינו של הפה ושני דיבורים בשמאלו, נשרשים בב׳ לחיים - עליון ותחתון. יוצאין ויורדין עד הטבור.

From the mouth of *Adam Kadmon,* ten interior, and ten encircling *Sephirot* came out; they were of the aspect of the lower *Ta'amim.* They returned inside the mouth to be completed, and came out again, they are called "returning lights". These lights came out from the same conduit, intermingled; and this is how the concept of *Keli* came to be. They spread down until the navel, but in one unique *Keli*. Since the ears and nose have two separate channels, their respective encircling and interior lights did not join, and thus stayed at a distance of each other. The mouth being one single channel, a *Keli* was needed to hold the interior lights, and to separate them from the more tenuous encircling lights.

d) *Mal'hut* came out[35] first, followed by *Z'A,* and than the others [*Sephirot* until *Keter*]. The force [the consistence] of the *Keli* was absorbed in them[36].	ד. יצאו ראשונה, מלכות בתחלה, וז״א אחריה, וכן כולם. וכח הכלי בלוע בהם.
The most tenuous [37] returned and entered [38] , *Keter* first, followed by the others. The rest [which did not return] thickened, and a *Keli* was made from the sparks that fell there from	הדק שבהם חזר ונכנס, כתר בתחלה וכולם אחריו. נתעבה הנשאר, ונעשה כלי מניצוצות שנפלו בו מהכאת אור חזרתו של עליון ורשימו של תחתון.

---

[35] From the mouth of *Adam Kadmon*
[36] The lights of the mouth of *Adam Kadmon*
[37] Of the lights
[38] In the mouth of *Adam Kadmon*

the collision of the returning higher light, with the trace [39] of the lower [light].

At first, they were all [of the aspect of] Nefashot. They gained from each other by coming out, and by returning; each one as it deserved, until the second encircling[40]. *Keter* stayed in the mouth of A`K, the nine remaining [*Sephirot*] came out, until *Mal'hut* was left as a *Keli* without light.

בראשונה היו כלם נפשות. הרויחו זה מזה ביציאתם וכן בחזרתם, כל אחד כראוי לו, עד מקיף שני. נשאר הכתר בפה דא״ק, ושאר התשעה יצאו, עד שנמצאת מלכות כלי בלי אור.

All the *Kelim* made one [unique] *Keli*, but with ten gradations. This is the [world of] Ha'Akudim.[41]

כל הכלים כלי אחד, אלא שעשר שנתות יש לו, זה עקודים.

Similar to the lights which have two aspects; interior and encircling, the *Keli* also has two aspects; interior and exterior. When the *Sephirot* came out the first time from the mouth, each one had its own place, but in one unique *Keli*; this is called the world of *Ha'Akudim* [the attached]. They returned to their origin in the mouth but not completely, each one leaving

---

[39] Each light when ascending, leaves a trace (imprint)
[40] For *Mal'hut* only
[41] Attached

its trace. Only the most tenuous part of the lights returned, the ones that remained thickened, but were still illuminated by their own part that ascended. The lights strike each other and produced sparks, which formed the *Kelim* for the more tenuous lights that had returned the second time. When the light of *Keter* went back up, it did not come out again; *'Hokhma* came out and took its place, *Binah* took the place of *'Hokhma*, and so on, until *Mal'hut* was left with no light, like a "non luminous mirror". (ספקלריא   דלא   נהרא).

This is considered as an annulment, but not as important as the one in *'Olam Hanikudim*, as we will see latter on.

Second chapter

The lights of the eyes, the breaking of the *Kelim*

Introduction

New lights, of the aspect of BaN, emerged from the eyes of Adam Kadmon. When they came out, they found Kelim to contain them. The first three Kelim were able to retain their lights, but the seven lower Kelim could not, and broke. The lights fell, yet stayed in the world of Atsilut, and the Kelim fell in the lower worlds. This is called 'Olam Hanikudim (the world of points).

a) The vowels of *SaG* being ready to come out, *SaG* assembled his own *MaH* and *BaN* [42] , and [the general] *MaH* and *BaN* with them, from the navel and up. It then spread there a curtain [a limit], starting in the front at the level of his chest, and extending down to his rear until the level of his navel.

From *BaN; Sephirot* ascended and came out trough the eyes [of *Adam* Kadmon]: ten [*Sephirot*] from the right, and ten from the left. They [the *Kelim*] came out from the navel, and downward. They [the *Sephirot*] took from the higher lights, *KHB* [43] [received from the lights] of the ears, nose and mouth that were on the beard of the chin, and the rest [the seven lower *Sephirot*

א. עמדו נקודותיו לצאת,
אסף ס״ג המ״ה וב״ן שלו,
ומ״ה וב״ן עמהם,
מן הטבור ולמעלה;
ופרש שם מסך,
מתחיל מלפניו בחזה,
ומשפע ויורד מאחריו,
עד כנגד הטבור.

ומן הב״ן עלו ויצאו מן העינים
עשר ספירות מן הימין, ועשר מן
השמאל.
יצאו וירדו מן הטבור ולמטה,
ולקחו אור ממה שלמעלה:
כח״ב מאח״פ בשבלתה של זקן,
והשאר מן הפה משם ולמטה.

---

[42] *MaH* of *SaG* and *BaN* of *SaG*
[43] *Keter, 'Hokhma* and *Binah*

received from the lights] of the mouth and lower [the beard on the chin].

From the inside [of *Adam Kadmon*], *BaN* descended, cleaved out at their level [of the lights of the eyes that went down] and shone outwards through his skin [of *Adam Kadmon*]. From the navel and the *Yesod* [of *Adam Kadmon*] the light divided to *Keter*, *'Hokhma* and *Binah*, the remaining [the seven lower *Sephirot*, received from the lights] of the toes.

ומבפנים ירד ובקע ב"ן כנגדם,
והאיר דרך עורו לחוץ.
מן הטבור ומן היסוד
נחלקת אור לכתר ולחו"ב,
והשאר מאצבעותיהם של רגלים.

The three first ones were repaired, facing each other, the remaining [seven lower *Sephirot*] were one under the other.

נמצא:
ג' ראשונות מתוקנים זה כנגד זה,
והשאר זה תחת זה.

b) Ten *Kelim* came out first, and afterwards, their lights. The lights went down to *Keter*, *'Hokhma* and *Binah* and were accepted; but by the seven lower ones, they

ב. יצאו עשרה כלים בראשונה,
ואורותיהם אח"כ.
ירדו האורות לכח"ב וקבלום;
לז"ת ולא קבלום.
ירדו כליהם למטה,
ואורותיהם עלו למקומם.

were not accepted. Their *Kelim* went down [to *Beriah*, *Yetsirah* and *'Asiah*], and their lights ascended to their place [in *Atsilut*].

On them, it is written: "And these are the kings who reigned in the land of Edom, before reigned a king over the children of Israel" (Bereshit, 36, 31).

ועליהם הוא אומר (בראשית לו, לא):

"ואלה המלכים אשר מלכו בארץ אדום לפני מלך מלך לבני ישראל".

After the diffusion of the lights of *'AV* of *SaG* from the ears, nose and mouth, the other lights of *SaG* needed to come out also. Inside of *Adam Kadmon*, *SaG* gathered its own aspects of *MaH* and *BaN* together with the general *MaH* and *BaN* of *Adam Kadmon*. It brought them up above the navel and put a veil as a separation. Its[44] lights of *BaN*, which are of the aspect of the *Nekudim*, came out with the general *BaN* through the eyes; ten encircling *Sephirot* from the right eye, and ten interior from the left eye, they descended lower than the navel. These lights are not visible above the navel because the lights of the ears, nose and mouth extend to that point.

Each one of these *Sephirot* had its own *Keli*, but only the three first ones: *Keter*, *'Hokhma* and *Binah*, were structured in the three-column order: B [K] H. However, the seven lower *Sephirot*

---

[44] Of *SaG*

were aligned one under the other in a straight line, and not ready for the guidance of kindness, rigor and mercy.

Until here, were the first emanations to create the worlds of *Ha'Akudim* [attached] and *HaNekoudim* [spotted], which are a preparation for the world of *Atsilut*. Next, we will see the unfolding of *Atsilut* and the lower worlds, which are the source of existence for the physical worlds, the possibility of reward, punishment, and evil.

c) Ten *Sephirot* [of *Nekudim*] to be divided into six *Partsufim* [in *Atsilut*], and from them, four worlds: *Atsilut*, *Beriah*, *Yetsirah* and *'Asiah*. From their extremity [of these levels][45] comes out evil, as it is said: "I form the light, and create darkness; I make peace, and create evil". (Isaiah, 45, 7)	ג. עשר ספירות עומדות ליחלק בששה פרצופים, ומהם נעשו ד' עולמות – אבי"ע ומסופם יוצא הרע, שנאמר (ישעיה מה, ז): "יוצר אור ובורא חושך עושה שלום ובורא רע".
The sparks have no attachments between them. As it is said: "A whisperer separates close friends" (Mich.16, 28)	זיקין ניצוצים אין ביניהם חיבור, שנאמר (משלי טז, כח): "ונרגן מפריד אלוף".
And for the wicked he said:	וברשעים הוא אומר (תהלים צב,

---

[45] *Mal'hut* of *'Asiah*

"All the evil doers shall be scattered:" (Tehilim,92, 10)

: (י

"יתפרדו כל פועלי און".

But for the saintly what does he say:
"And G-d will be king on all the land, on this day G-d will be One and His Name One" (Zachariah, 14, 9)

אבל בקדושה מה הוא אומר
(זכריה יד, ט):
"והיה ה' למלך על כל הארץ ביום ההוא יהיה ה' אחד ושמו אחד" –

Because the *Tikun* of everything; is by the unity [*Yi'hud*].

שתיקון הכל ביחוד

d) In the beginning, all the parts [of the *Kelim*] were equal. The lights came out but were not accepted [by Z'aT [46]], they [the *Kelim*] broke and fell. The finest [of the lights] were concealed, and the best of those remaining [of the *Kelim*] descended to *Beriah*, the rest to *Yetsirah*

ד. בתחלה היו כל החלקים שוים.
באו האורות ולא קיבלום, נשברו ונפלו.
נגנז המעולה שבהם,
ומן הנשאר ירד הטוב שבו לבריאה,
ושלאחריו ליצירה,
ושלאחריו לעשיה.

---

[46] *Zain Tahtonim* – The seven lower *Sephirot*
[47] From the three worlds of *Beriah*, *Yetsirah* and *'Asiah*, were made the four worlds of *Atsilut*, *Beriah*, *Yetsirah* and *'Asiah*
[48] *Mal'hut* of the second *'Asiah*

and *'Asiah*.

When they [the *Kelim*] came back and were repaired, four were made of three[47]. The second *'Asiah* is lower than the first, and from its extremity[48], evil comes out. As the prophet said: "Behold, I will make you small among the nations; you shall be greatly despised" (Ovadia, 1, 2)	כשחזרו ונתקנו, נעשה מג' ד'. נמצאת עשיה השניה תחתונה מהראשונה. ומסופה הרע יוצא, הוא שהנביא אמר (עובדיה א, ב): "קטן נתתיך בגוים בזוי אתה מאד"

Here, a world, is a notion of category of existence, influence, and power of guidance. The first world to unfold from *Adam Kadmon* is called *Atsilut*; the world of emanation, where there is no existence of the separated[49], and no *Sitra A'hra*[50], even at its lowest levels[51]. The second is *Beriah*; the world of creation, the beginning of existence for the separated; it is the world of the souls. The third is *Yetsirah*; the world of formation, the world of the angels. The fourth is *'Asiah*; the world of action, the world of physical existence.

From the extremity of *'Asiah* evil begins. When the Emanator decided that there would be evil in this world, it needed to

---

[49] Distinct beings: Souls, angels and physical creatures
[50] Negative side (evil)
[51] Of *Atsilut*

have a root, with the concept of *Keli*; notion of limit and rigor, this root was revealed from the last level of the *Sephirot* [*Mal'hut* of *'Asiah*].

---

e) Which [52] ones went down? The seven lower ones[53] and the rears of *'Hokhma* and *Binah*. The seven lower went down to *Beriah*, the rears of *'Hokhma* and *Binah* went down to the place of *Z'uN* in *Atsilut*, the rears of *'Hokhma* in front, and those of *Binah* in the back [back to back]. The seven lower ones broke, but the rears of *'Hokhma* and *Binah* did not; they only fell. The rears of *NHY* of *Keter* were also damaged with them.

In every *Partsuf*, the seven lower [*Sephirot*] broke, the rears of *'Hokhma* and *Binah* fell, and the rears of *NHY* of *Keter* were damaged.
Of which *Partsufim*? The ones that will come after[54].

ה. מי הם היורדים ?
ז״ת, ואחוריהם של חו״ב;
אלא שז״ת ירדו לבריאה,
ואחוריהם של חו״ב למקום זו״ן
שבאצילות :
אחורי חכמה מלפניהם
ואחורי בינה מאחוריהם.
ז״ת נשברו ;
ואחורי חו״ב לא נשברו אלא נפלו ;
ואחורי נה״י של כתר נפגמו עמהם.

נמצאו :
ז״ת שבכל פרצוף שבורים,
ואחורי חו״ב נפולים,
ושל נה״י של כתר פגומים.
באיזה פרצופין דברו ?
באותן שלאחר כך

---

[52] *Kelim*

f) How did they [*Z'aT*] fall?

ו. כיצד נפלו ?

The first one [to fall] was *Da'at*, it received seven lights [from *Z'aT* of *Nekudim*] but could not hold them; it broke and fell. Its *Keli* [fell] to *Da'at* of *Beriah*, and its light to *Mal'hut* of *Atsilut*.

ראשון שבכולם **דעת,**
קבל ז' אורות, ולא עמד בהם,
נשבר ונפל,
כליו בדעת דבריאה,
ואור שלו במלכות דאצילות.

Afterwards, *'Hesed* received six lights; it broke and fell. Its *Keli* fell to *Binah* of *Beriah*, and its light to *Yesod* of *Atsilut*.

קבל **חסד** אחריו ששה אורות נשבר
ונפל,
כליו בבינה דבראה,
ואור שלו ביסוד דאצילות.

Gevurah received in the same way; it broke and fell. Its *Keli* fell to *'Hokhma* of

קבלה **גבורה** על דרך זה, נשברה
ונפלה,
כליה בחכמה דבריאה,

---

[53] *Sephirot*

[54] Being still in the world of *Nekudim*, the concept of *Partsuf* does not exist yet, we are then talking about the world of *Tikun*

[55] Being of the same column, (central)

[56] The light of *Daat*

[57] Of *Daat*

[58] Being of the same column, (left)

[59] The light of *Gevurah*

[60] Of *Gevurah*

[61] Being of the same column, (right)

[62] The light of *'Hesed*

[63] Of *'Hesed*

Beriah, and its light to *Netsah* and *Hod* of *Atsilut.*

ואורה בנ״ה דאצילות.

Tiferet received in the same way; it broke and fell. Its *Keli* fell to *Keter* of *Beriah,* and its light remained in place. The *Keli* of *Keter* extended[55] and received it[56], the light of *Da'at* went up between them, and its *Keli*[57] fell a second time, [but now] to *Mal'hut* of *Beriah.*

קבל **תפארת** על דרך זה, נשבר ונפל,
כליו בכתר דבריאה,
ואור שלו עמד במקומו.
נתפשט כלי הכתר וקיבלו.
ואור הדעת עלה ביניהם,
ונפל כלי שלו שניה עד המלכות דבריאה.

The lights went out to [the *Kelim* of] *Netsah* and *Hod,* there, they found the light of *Gevurah* that had fallen, [the *Keli* of] *Binah* extended[58] and received it[59], and its *Keli*[60] fell a second time, [but now] to *Yesod* of *Beriah. Netsah* and *Hod* received and broke; their *Kelim* [fell] to *Netsah* and *Hod* of *Beriah,* their lights went up to the *Keli* of *Binah.*

יצאו האורות לנ״ה.
מצאו שם אור הגבורה שנפלה.
נתפשטה הבינה וקבלתו,
וירד כליה שניה עד היסוד דבריאה.
קבלו נ״ה, ונשברו,
ונפל כלים בנ״ה דבריאה,
ואורם עלה לכליה של בינה.

The lights went out to [the *Keli* of] *Yesod,* there, they found the light of *'Hesed.*

יצאו האורות ליסוד,
ומצאו שם אורו של חסד.
נתפשטה החכמה וקבלתו,

'Hokhma extended [61] and received it[62], and its *Keli*[63] fell a second time [but now] to *Tiferet* of *Beriah*.

נפל כליו שניה עד התפארת.

Yesod received, broke and fell; its *Keli* [fell] to *Gevurah* of *Beriah*, and its light went up to *Keter*.

קבל **היסוד**, נשבר ונפל,
כליו לגבורה דבריאה,
ואור שלו עלה לכתר.

Mal'hut received, broke and fell; its *Keli* [fell] to *'Hesed* of *Beriah*, and its light went up to *Keter*.

קיבלה **המלכות**, נשברה ונפלה,
כליה לחסד דבריאה,
ואור שלה עלה לכתר.

This is the order of the breaking of the seven lower [*Sephirot*]. It is from them that the worlds of *Beriah*, *Yetsirah* and *'Asiah* were prepared, and constructed.

זה סדר שבירתם של ז״ת,
שבהם הוכנו ונעשו בי״ע.

g) The descent of the rears of *'Hokhma* and *Binah* was consequent to the breaking of the [seven] lower ones:

ז. ירידת אחוריים של חו״ב
לפי שבירתם של תחתונות.

'Hokhma and *Binah*[64] were face to face. [When] *Da'at*

חו״ב - פנים בפנים.

---

[64] In the beginning

broke, the *'Hasadim* and *Gevurot* of *'Hokhma* and *Binah* fell into their body[65], they turned [66] [back to back]; so as not to look at each other.

נשבר **דעת**,
ונפלו חו"ג שבחו"ב בגוף,
חזרו שלא להסתכל זה בזה.

'Hesed broke; the rears [*NHY*] of *Abah* went down to *Yesod* [of *Abah*]; his rears [67] turned from facing *Imah*.

נשבר **חסד**,
ירדו אחוריו של אבא עד היסוד,
והפך אחוריו לפני אימא.

Gevurah broke; the rears of *Imah* went down to *Yesod* [of *Imah*], they both turned[68] back to back.

נשברה **גבורה**,
ירדו אחוריה של אימא עד היסוד,
חזרו שניהם אחור באחור.

The third of *Tiferet* broke; the rears of the *Yesod*s of *Abah* and *Imah* went down.

נשבר **שלישו של תפארת**,
ירדו אחורי יסודיהם של או"א.

Tiferet broke completely; the *'Hasadim* and *Gevurot* of *Israel Saba* and *Tevunah*

גמר **ת"ת** להשבר,
ירדו חו"ג שביסו"ת בגופם,
חזרו שלא להסתכל זה בזה.

---

[65] From their heads, their *'Hasadim* and *Gevurot* fell into their bodies
[66] The heads of *Abah* and *Imah*
[67] Of his body, his head had turned already
[68] *Abah* and *Imah* are now back to back
[69] *ISOT*
[70] Of *ISOT*
[71] Of *ISOT*
[72] *NHY* of *Keter*

descended in their bodies, they turned[69] so as not to look at each other.

Netsah and Hod broke; the rears of ISOT descended until Yesod.

נשברו נ"ה,
ירדו אחוריהם של יסו"ת עד
היסוד.

Yesod broke; the rears of their Yesods[70] fell.

נשבר **היסוד**,
נפלו אחורי יסודיהם.

Mal'hut broke; the rear of their crowns[71] [surrounding their Yesods] fell, and the damage to [the rears of] NHY of Keter was completed. It is by them[72] that the 'Hasadim and Gevurot enter 'Hokhma and Binah.

נשברה **מלכות**,
ירדו אחורי עטרותיהם.
ונשלם פגמם של נה"י דכתר,
שבהן נכנסין חו"ג בחו"ב.

When the Sephirot of BaN came out from the eyes of Adam Kadmon, the first three Sephirot - KHB, took strength from the lights of the ears, nose and mouth of A'K, and were able to stand in three columns. It is only when the column of mercy stands between the columns of kindness and rigor, that can attach and bind together. The seven lower Sephirot who only took from the lights of the mouth, could not stand in this order and formed a single descending line. This imperfect arrangement is the first origin of the Sitra A'hra[73] or "evil".

---

[73] Other side

This type of existence could not come to be from a perfect source; it had to originate from a defective state.

The *Sephirot* of *Keter*, *'Hokhma* and *Binah* received and contained their lights, because they were in the three-column arrangement. However, a minor part could not contain the lights, and fell without breaking.

In the world of *Akudim,* when the *Sephirot* emerged from the mouth, the lights came out first, and then one unique *Keli* was formed. However, in this emanation of the lights from the eyes, first the individual *Keli* for each *Sephira* came out, and then the lights.

The *Kelim* of the seven lower *Sephirot* could not contain their lights; they broke and descended to the world of *Beriah.* The lights also fell, but stayed in *Atsilut.*

The roots of all the created are in the seven lower *Sephirot* [*Z'aT*], the *G'aR*[74] are like a crown on the *Z'aT*[75] to repair and direct them. In the *G'aR* there is not really a notion of damage, they are above men's deeds, and are not affected by their sins. The inferior part of *G'aR*, which did not contain their lights, corresponds to what is needed for the guidance of *Z'aT*, if it

---

[74] *Shalosh Rishonot* (three first ones), *Keter*, *'Hokhma* and *Binah*
[75] *Zain Tahtonot* (seven lower)

had contained them[76], the Z'aT would not have broken, and the notions of *Kilkul* and *Tikun*[77] would not have existed.

The breaking of the *Kelim* caused a descent of the world of *Atsilut*. However, *KHB* remained in what is called the "first *Atsilut*". The seven lower *Sephirot* fell in the higher parts of *Beriah,* which became the *Atsilut* of today, *Beriah* fell in the higher part of *Yetsirah,* which became the *Beriah* of today, *Yetsirah* in the higher parts of *'Asiah,* which became the *Yetsirah* of today, *'Asiah* fell even lower and became the *'Asiah* of today. From the end of *'Asiah*, the *Sitra A'hra* came out.

h) The 288 sparks are lights from the four *'AV*: *'AV* of *'AV*, *'AV* of *SaG*, *'AV* of *MaH* and *'AV* of *BaN*, which descended with the broken *Kelim* to sustain them.	ח. ורפי״ח ניצוצין של אור מארבעה ע״ב דעסמ״ב ירדו עם הנשברים לקיימם.
What descended did so as a result of the descent of the Malkin[78] (kings), and what returned and rose again did so because of their return.	כל היורד - מירידתם של מלכים הוא יורד, וכל החוזר ועולה - מחזרתם הוא חוזר.

---

[76] The lights
[77] Damage and repair
[78] The seven kings of Edom that died, correspond to the Z'aT that broke

At the end of things what does he say: "And the light of the moon will be as the light of the sun... When G-d will dress the wounds of His people and heal its bruise. " (Isaiah. 30 .26)	ובסופן של דברים מה הוא אומר (ישעיה ל, כו): "והיה אור הלבנה כאור החמה" ואומר (שם): "ביום חבוש ה' את שבר עמו ומחץ מכתו ירפא"
A recovery which is not followed by a blow. As he said: "I will erase the sin of this land in one day." (Zachariah 3. 9). And he said:	רפואה שאין אחריה מכה; ואומר (זכריה ג, ט): "ומשתי את עון הארץ ההיא ביום אחד";
"And G-d will be king on all the land, on this day G-d will be One and His Name One. " (Zachariah 14. 9.).	ואומר (שם יד, ט): "והיה ה' למלך על כל הארץ ביום ההוא יהיה ה' אחד ושמו אחד"

To sustain the *Kelim* after they broke, 288 sparks of the lights came down as well, because a connection to their original lights was needed to keep them alive. They[79] correspond to the four *'AV* of *ASMB*[80], 4 x 72 = 288. This fall of the *Kelim,* is also called their death.

---

[79] The sparks
[80] *'AV, SaG, MaH, BaN*

It is important to understand that all that happens in our world, is similar to what occurred in this fall. The separation between *G'aR*, which is considered the *Mo'hin*[81], and *Z'aT* - the body, is like the death of a man, when his soul departs and goes up, while his body descends into the earth. The *Or* that gives life to the *Keli* is comparable to the soul that keeps the body alive. However, when a man dies and his soul separates from his body, the latter will remain with the "*Habela Degarmi*" הבלא (דגרמי), which like the 288 sparks, will allow the conservation of the body from the time the soul has left him, until the resurrection.

The goal of all the works, deeds and prayers of men in this existence, is to help and participate in the ascent of these sparks to their origin. At the completion of this *Tikun* of unification between the fallen sparks and their *Kelim*, it will be the time of the resurrection of the dead and the arrival of Moshia'h.

---

[81] Brain or intelligence, the three *Sephirot, Keter, 'Hokhma, Binah*

Third chapter

The construction of the *Partsufim 'Atik, Arikh Anpin, Abah and Imah*

Introduction

Other lights, of the aspect of MaH, came out through the forehead of Adam Kadmon. The union between the lights of MaH; which represent mercy, with the ones of BaN, which represent rigor, made the Tikun of the broken Sephirot. This Tikun is also the arrangement of the Sephirot in three columns, which will allow the beginning of the construction of the first Partsufim: 'Atik Yomin, Arikh Anpin, Abah and Imah.

a) *MaH*[82] came out through the forehead [of *Adam Kadmon*], it selected and made from all the broken *Kelim* [83] five *Partsufim* [*Arikh Anpin, Abah, Imah, Zeir Anpin* and *Nukvah*], and *'Atik* above them, and from the rears of *Abah* and *Imah* [84] [it made] *Ya'acov* and *Leah*.

א. יצא מ״ה מן המצח, בירר לו ועשה מכל שבריהם של כלים חמשה פרצופים, ועתיק שעל גביהם, ומאחוריהם של אוי״א - יעקב ולאה.

From *Keter* of *MaH*, and from half of *Keter*[85] of *BaN*, and from what was needed from the rest[86], *'Atik*[87] was realized.

כתר דמ״ה וחצי כתר דב״ן, ומן השאר הראוי לו לעתיק.

From *'Hokhma* of *MaH*, and from half of *Keter*[88] of *BaN*,

חכמה דמ״ה וחצי כתרו של ב״ן, ומהשאר הראוי לו זה אי״א.

---

[82] The ten *Sephirot* of *MaH*
[83] *Z'aT* of *BaN*
[84] Their *NHY* that fell, but still in *Atsilut*
[85] Five superior *Sephirot* of *Keter*
[86] Of the *Sephirot*
[87] *Atik* is the *Mal'hut* of *Adam Kadmon*, that enters *Atsilut* to attach it to him
[88] Five lower *Sephirot* of *Keter*
[89] By the union of the *Sephirot* of the masculine aspect – *MaH*, and the feminine aspect – *BaN*
[90] *Duchrin* and *Nukvin* - Aramaic for masculine and feminine. The *Partsuf* is repaired by the union of the masculine and feminine aspects of the *Partsuf* superior to him

and from what was needed from the rest, *Arikh Anpin* was realized.

From *Binah* of *MaH,* and from *'Hokhma* and *Binah* of *BaN,* and from what was needed from the rest; *Abah* and *Imah* were realized.

בינה דמ״ה וחו״ב של ב״ן,
ומהשאר הראוי להם - או״א.

From the seven lower *Sephirot* of *MaH,* and from the seven *Sephirot* of *BaN, Zeir Anpin* was realized.

וי״ק דמ״ה ווי״ק של ב״ן - ז״א.

From *Mal'hut* of *MaH,* and from *Mal'hut* of *BaN, Nukvah* was realized.

מלכותו של מ״ה ומלכותו של ב״ן -
נוק׳.

Their *Tikun* [rectification - arrangement] is achieved by the masculine and feminine[89] principles. They are repaired by *D'uN*[90]; during the *Zivug,*[91] the gestation, the birth, and the growth.

תיקונם בזכר ונקבה.
ומדו״ן הם נתקנים :
בזיווג, עיבור, לידה, וגדלות.

---

[91] Union

After the breaking of the *Kelim* and the separation from their lights, it was necessary for the guidance of the world, that reparation be done. From the forehead of *Adam Kadmon* came out ten *Sephirot* of the aspect of the name of *MaH;* corresponding to the masculine - reparation. In contrast, the *Sephirot* of *BaN* correspond to the feminine aspect - rigor, and are the root of deterioration. These two aspects[92] are necessary for the guidance of justice, and to give man the possibility of free choice.

The *Kilkul*[93] was caused by the disposition of the *Sephirot* in a straight line (one under the other), instead of the three-column arrangement. The *Tikun*[94] is the union of the *Sephirot* of *MaH* and *BaN* in complex arrangements, as to allow the feminine *BaN* to be repaired by the masculine *MaH,* and for the *Sephirot* to stand in the three-column arrangement of kindness, justice and mercy. The name of *BaN* represents rigor, while *MaH* is mercy. Creation based on rigor was not possible; if man was to be judged on this basis he would not survive. The name of *MaH* is the *Miluim*[95] of א, which is a (ו) (*vav*) line in the middle [mercy] that unites two י (*yud*) [kindness and rigor].

With the proper order of the *Sephirot* in place, various configurations that are called *Partsufim* [96] completed the creation. Some *Partsufim* are masculine and bestow kindness, others are feminine and bestow rigor. By their union, different

---

[92] *MaH* and *BaN*
[93] Damage - deterioration
[94] Reparation
[95] For the total of 45
[96] Configuration of one, or more *Sephirot* acting in coordination

equilibriums of these two forces [97], make the guidance. Complete rigor will be the destruction of anything not perfect, while complete kindness will permit everything without restriction. Thus we see that everything that is, and happens, is always composed of a variable measure and balance of these two forces.

b) The *Zivug* [98], in what manner [is it done]? [First] The *Nukvah* [of the upper *Partsuf*] brings up *Mayim Nukvin* [99] [feminine desire], which make the selection of the *Kelim*, and then in return; the lights [100] of *MaH* come down.	ב. בזיווג כיצד ? מעלה נוק׳ מ״ן - בירוריהם של כלים, ויורדים כנגדם אורותיו של מ״ה.
They stand [101] in *Nukvah* [102], and are repaired in her interior; this corresponds to the gestation ('Ibur).	עומדים בנוק׳ ונתקנים בה – זה **העיבור**.
They [the lights and the *Kelim*] come out [103] to their positions; this is the birth	יצאו למקומם - זו היא **לידה**.

---

[97] Kindness and rigor
[98] Union
[99] Feminine waters
[100] *Mayim Duchrin* (masculine waters)
[101] *Mayim Nukvin* and *Mayim Duchrin*
[102] In her *Yesod*
[103] After the time of the gestation, their details are distinct

(Leida). When the lower *Partsuf*[104] dresses the higher *Partsuf* and grows to his size; this is the growth (*Gadlut*).	הלביש תחתון לעליון והגיע לשיעורו - זה **הגדלות**.
At first he suckles from the upper *Partsuf* (to gather strength), as needed for his growth, and once grown and clothed, he becomes independent.	יונק מתחלה - שהוא צריך לעליונו. השלים והלביש - עושה את שלו.

All the *Tikunim* of the *Partsufim* (masculine and feminine) are acheived by way of *Zivug* (union), gestation and birth. During the *Zivug*, the lights of *MaH* needed for the *Tikun* are drawn to the lights of *BaN*, and are kept in the upper *Nukvah*[105]. During the gestation, inside of Nukvah, they are arranged and completed until there is nothing more to add. When it is totally repaired, the *Partsuf* is revealed, and this is the birth. There is afterwards the suckling, and finally the growth, so that the *Partsuf* will be fully independent (this is explained in more details in chapter six, which deals with the details of the *Zivugim*).

c) The ascent of the Malkin [106] [from *Beriah* to *Atsilut*] is of forty days:	ג. עליתם של מלכים ארבעים יום. כיצד ?

---

[104] Now the lights and *Kelim* are arranged as a *Partsuf*
[105] The *Nukvah* above that gives birth to the *Partsuf*
[106] The *Kelim* of *Z'aT* that broke

Ten days: *'Hesed* and *Netsah,* to *Netsah* of *Atsilut.*	עשרה ימים חסד ונצח לנצחו של אצילות.
Ten days: *Da'at* and *Tiferet,* to his *Yesod*[107].	ועשרה - דעת ותפארת ליסודו.
Ten days: *Gevurah* and *Hod,* to his *Hod*[108].	עשרה - גבורה והוד להודו.
Ten days: *Yesod* and *Mal'hut,* to his *Mal'hut*[109].	ועשרה - יסוד ומלכות למלכותו.

d) *'Atik* is repaired by *D'uN*[110]. His *MaH* is his front masculine side, his *BaN*; his rear feminine side. The face of *MaH* his front, the face of *BaN* his rear[111]; thus *'Atik* is all face.	ד. נתקן עתיק דו"ן. מ"ה שלו - זכר לפניו, ובי"ן שלו - נוק' לאחוריו. פני מ"ה לפניו, ופני ב"ן לאחוריו. נמצא עתיק כולו פנים.
Arikh Anpin is repaired by *D'uN;* masculine[112] on his right, feminine[113] on his left.	נתקן אריך דו"ן, הזכר בימינו והנוקבא בשמאלו.
The *Tikun* of *Arikh Anpin* is from the *Zivug* of *'Atik.* The *Tikun* of *'Atik* is from the *Zivug* of higher than him.	תיקונו של א"א מזיווגו של עתיק. תיקונו של עתיק מזיווג עליון ממנו.

---

[107] Of *Atsilut*

[108] Of *Atsilut*

[109] Of *Atsilut*

[110] By the zivoug of higher than him (*'AV* and *SaG* of *Adam Kadmon*)

[111] His *MaH* and *BaN* are back to back

[112] His aspect of *MaH*

[113] His aspect of *BaN*

'Atik was constructed by the Zivug of 'AV and SaG of Adam Kadmon. His MaH corresponds to the masculine principle, his BaN to the feminine, he is called 'Atik and his Nukvah. His Nukvah is never separated from him, her back attached to his back, 'Atik is thus all face; the face of BaN corresponding to his back, the face of MaH to his front. By the Zivug of 'Atik, Arikh[114] and his Nukvah were built, and from their Zivug[115] Abah and Imah were built. Arikh Anpin is the first Partsuf in Atsilut and the root of all the others, which are his branches.

| e) By the Zivug of Arikh Anpin; Abah and Imah are arranged, this one masculine and this one feminine, and from their Zivug[116]; Z'A and Nukvah are built. The Yesod of 'Atik ends in the chest[117] of Arikh Anpin,[118] the 'Hasadim and Gevurot are revealed from it[119]. | ה. מזיווגו של א״א נתקנים אוי״א, זה זכר וזה נקבה, ומזיווגם - זו״ן. יסודו של עתיק כלה בחזהו של אי״א, וחו״ג מתגלים ממנו. |
| The Gevurot came out[120] first, being pushed out by | יצאו הגבורות ראשונה מפני דוחקם של חסדים, |

---

[114] His right side is masculine, his left, feminine
[115] Of Arich Anpin and his Nukvah
[116] Of Abah and Imah
[117] Tiferet
[118] According to the Hishtalshelout (development) but not for the clothing, where it is in the Yesod of Arich Anpin
[119] Yesod of Atik
[120] From the Yesod of Atik

the 'Hasadim; they surrounded Yesod [of 'Atik] on all sides. The 'Hasadim came out; their halves[121] to the right, and pushed all the Gevurot to its left [of Yesod]. Their halves [122] descended from the chest and lower, and the 'Hasadim also descended to appease them. Therefore, there are two and a half 'Hasadim revealed and two and a half covered, which are spreading their lights[123] to the outside.	סבבו את היסוד לכל רוח. יצאו החסדים חצים לימין, ודחו את הגבורות כולם לשמאלו. ירדו חצים מן החזה ולמטה, והחסדים יורדים כנגדם למתקם. נמצאו: ב' חסדים וחצי מגולים, וב' חסדים וחצי מכוסים, מוציאים הארתם לחוץ.
From the 'Hasadim, Abah and Israel Saba came out to the right of Arikh, and from the Gevurot, Imah and Tevunah came out to his left. Imah and Tevunah; the legs of one [Imah] in the head of the other [Tevunah], it is not the same for Abah and Israel	יצאו מן החסדים אבא וישראל סבא לימין של אריך, ומן הגבורות אימא ותבונה לשמאלו. אימא ותבונה - רגליה של זו בראשה של זו; מה שאינו כן אבא וי"ס. ששני חצאיהם של גבורות מגולים כאחד, וחצים של חסדים מכוסים ביסוד.

---

[121] Two and a half

[122] Two and a half of the Gevurot

[123] From Yesod they project though a veil

[124] Which are not attached

Saba[124], because two halves of *Gevurot* are revealed as one, while half of *'Hasadim* are covered in *Yesod*.

---

f) *Abah* and *Imah* are the two *Mo'hin* [125] [brains] of *Atsilut;* they dress the two arms ['*Hesed* and *Gevurah*] of *Arikh*. They are constructed from *MaH* and *BaN*, and built [126] by the lights of *Arikh*.

ו. אוי״א - שני מוחותיו של אצילות מלבישים זרועותיו של אי״א. בנינם ממ״ה וב״ן, ותיקוניהם מאורותיו של אריך.

From the three parts [127] of the arms ['*Hesed* and *Gevurah* of *Arikh*], to their *HBD* [of *Abah* and *Imah*], and from *Tiferet* [of *Arikh*], to the rest of their body [of *Abah* and *Imah*]. From the first three parts of *HGT* [of *Arikh*], to make their *Mo'hin* as one, from the second parts to make their *HGT*, and from the third parts; their *NHY*.

מג׳ פרקיהם של זרועות לחב״ד שלהם, ומת״ת לשאר כל גופם. ומג׳ פרקים ראשונים של חג״ת לעשות מוחותיהם כאחד, מפרקים שניים לחג״ת שלהם, מפרקים שלישיים לנה״י שלהם.

---

[125] *'Hokhma* and *Binah*
[126] Their actions are influenced by the lights of *Arich*
[127] *'Hesed* and *Gevurah* have three parts each

| The first parts of the right [arm] is clothed in the head of *Abah*, at the same level [128] ; the left [arm] is clothed in *Imah*, the second [parts are clothed] in their *HGT*, and the third [parts] in their *NHY*. | פרקו הראשון של ימין מתלבש בראשו של אבא, כנגדו בשמאל באימא, שני לו בחג״ת של זה וזה, שלישי לו בנה״י, |
| *Tiferet* [of *Arikh*] is covered under them, until the chest. | והתי״ת נכסה תחתיהן מאליו עד החזה. |

Abah and *Imah* are the two *Partsufim* that came out from the aspects of *'Hokhma* and *Binah* of *Atsilut*. In reality, they were meant to dress *'Hokhma* and *Binah* of *Arikh Anpin*, but because of the breaking of the *Kelim*, they underwent a fall. From the arms [*'Hesed* and *Gevurah*] of *Arikh Anpin*, came out lights to build their *HBD*, and from *Tiferet* came out lights to build their bodies. This is a first emanation to build them together.

From the first parts of *'Hesed* and *Gevurah* of *Arikh*, will be constituted the *HBD* of *Abah* and *Imah*, from the second parts their *HGT*, and from the third parts their *NHY;* this is a second emanation to build them as separate *Partsufim*.

From the first part of *'Hesed*, for *HBD* of *Abah*, from the first part of *Gevurah*, for *HBD* of *Imah*, from their second parts;

---

[128] The first parts

their *HGT,* and from their third parts; their *NHY*; this is a third emanation for the *Halbasha* הלבשה (clothing).

| g) *Abah* and *Imah*, have *MaH* and *BaN* in them. When they[129] joined, *Abah* gave his *BaN* to *Imah,* and took her *MaH* for himself. Two *MaH* on the right: *Abah* and *Israel Saba* Two *BaN* on the left: *Imah* and *Tevunah.* | ז. אוייא - מייה ובייו בשניהם.
נתחברו זה בזה,
נתן אבא בייו שלו לאימא,
ונטל מייה שלה לעצמו.
שני מייה בימין - אבא וישייס,
שני בייו בשמאל - אימא ותבונה |

During the gestation inside *Nukvah* of *Arikh Anpin,* for the construction of *Abah* and *Imah, MaH* and *BaN* were given to them. Afterwards, *Abah* took all *MaH* for himself, and gave his *BaN* to *Imah.* Consequently, *Abah* had two aspects of *MaH:* the first and the second. From the first aspect of *MaH, Abah* was made, and from the second, *Israel Saba.* Similarly, from the first *BaN Imah* was made, and from the second, *Tevunah.*

| h) *ISOT*[130] how [are they constructed]? The Malhuts of *Abah* and *Imah* become distinct *Partsufim,* half of their *Tiferet,* and *NHY* [of *Abah* and *Imah*] dress | ח. ישסויית כיצד ?
מלכותם של אוייא נעשית פרצוף
לעצמה,
וחצי תיית ונהייי שלהם מלובשים
מוחים בתוכם |

---

[129] *Abah* and *Imah*
[130] *Israel Saba* and *Tevunah*

inside of them[131], as their *Mo'hin*.

Abah and *Imah* are completed again; from there and up[132]. *Abah* and *Imah* are at the level of the chest of *Arikh*, *ISOT* is at [the level of] his navel.	חזרו או״א להשתלם משם ולמעלה. נמצאו: או״א כלים בחזה של אי״א, יסו״ת בטבור שלו.
Abah and *Israel Saba*, [as] *Imah* and *Tevunah* are sometimes two [133], and sometimes one [134]; when they are joined one to the other.	אבא וי״ס אימא ותבונה – פעמים שנים, פעמים אחד – שהם מתחברים זה בזה.

When the *NHY* of *Abah* and *Imah* are given as *Mo'hin* to *ISOT*, new *NHY* are given to them[135] so that they will be complete *Partsufim* once again. They are four (*Abah*, *Israel Saba*, *Imah* and *Tevunah*), during the first growth of *Z'A*, and two (*Abah* and *Imah*), during his second growth when *ISOT* merge in them.

i) The *Mo'hin* of *Z'A* are from *Abah* and *Imah*, they	ט. מוחין של ז״א מאו״א, מלובשים בכלים שלהם, זהו

---

131 *Mal'hut - ISOT*
132 With new *NHY*
133 Two separate *Partsufim*
134 *Partsuf*
135 *Abah* and *Imah*

are clothed in their *Kelim*[136], this is the צלמ. How? The *Mal'hut* of the superior [*Partsuf*] is the interiority of the lower; the *Malhuts* of *Abah* and *Imah* are in *Z'A*. Her *NHY*[137] enter in him, her nine parts[138] in his nine limbs [of *Z'A*]; this is the צ. Her first seven [*KHBD HGT* of *Tevunah*] are encircling him on the outside; this is his ל מ.	הצל״ם. כיצד ? מלכותו של עליון פנימיות בתחתון – מלכותם של או״א בז״א. נה״י שבה נכנסים בתוכו, ט׳ פירקיהן בט׳ איבריו, זה צ׳. ושבע ראשונות שלה מקיפים עליו מבחוץ – לי מ׳ שלו.

The *Mo'hin* of *Z'A* are given to him by the *Zivug* of *Abah* and *Imah*. Depending on the state of growth of *Z'A*, they are from *ISOT*, or directly from *Abah* and *Imah*. A first part [*NHY*] of the *Mo'hin* enter inside the *Partsuf*, while the other two parts [*HGT* and *KHBD*] encircle him on the outside.

The *NHY* that enter, correspond to the צ

The *HGT* that surround him, correspond to the ל

The *KHBD* that encircle him, correspond to the מ

j) [When] *Abah* and *Imah*, [are separated from] *ISOT* [which] are two[139], *Z'A* is	י. או״א ישסו״ת - שנים, ז״א למטה מכולם, מוחיו מיסו״ת.

---

[136] Of *ISOT*, or *Abah* and *Imah*; depending on the state of growth of *Z'A*
[137] Of *Tevunah*
[138] *NHY* of *Tevunah* have three parts each
[139] *ISOT* 1 and *ISOT* 2

lower than all, and his
Mo'hin are from *ISOT*.

[When] Their Malhuts [140]
are his צלמ, this
corresponds to *ISOT* 2.
From their chest [of *ISOT*
2] and down [*NHY*], *Mo'hin*
are given to him [*Z'A*]. New
NHY are made for them[141],
extending and going down
his back to the level of his
chest, like a mother
covering her young.

מלכות שלהם צלם שלו,
אלו יסו״ת שניים.
מן החזה שלהם ולמטה ניתן לו
למוחין.
ונעשים כנגדם נה״י חדשים
לעצמם,
משתלשלים ויורדים מאחוריו עד
כנגד החזה,
כאם זו שרובצת על בניה.

From the chest [of *ISOT* 2]
and up [142], this is his למ;
corresponding to the first
growth. [*Gadlut* 1]

מן החזה ולמעלה : לי מי שלו,
זה גדלות ראשון.

k) [When] They [*Abah*,
Imah, and *ISOT*] are one,
and *Z'A* is under them, his
Mo'hin are [directly] from
Abah and *Imah*, and their

יא. נעשו אחד,
וז״א למטה מהם, מוחיו מאו״א,
מלכות שלהם צל״ם שלו,
אין כאן ישסו״ת אלא אחת.

---

[140] Of *ISOT*

[141] *ISOT* 2

[142] The *Sephirot* on top of *NHY* of *Tevunah* are his למ (his exterior *Mo'hin*)

Malhuts [143] are his צלם; there is then only one *ISOT*.	
From the chest and down[144] are his צ, the rest[145] are his למ; corresponding to the second growth. [*Gadlut* 2]	מן החזה ולמטה - צ׳ שלו, והשאר - ל׳ מ׳. הרי זה גדלות שני.

When *NHY* of *ISOT* 2 are clothed in *Z'A* as his *Mo'hin*; it is the first growth. But when *NHY* of *ISOT* 1 are clothed in him, it is considered as if *Abah* and *Imah* were clothed in him directly as *Mo'hin;* and this is the second growth.

1) The *Zivug* of *Abah* and *Imah* is constant, but the one of *ISOT* is occasional. The *Zivug* for the liveliness of the worlds is constant, but the one of the *Mo'hin* is occasional	יב. זיווג של או״א תדירי, ושל יסו״ת - לפרקים. זיווג חיות העולמות - תדירי, ושל מוחין - בזמנם.

For *Abah* and *Imah* there are two types of *Zivug:* the constant *Zivug* is called exterior, and is for the subsistence of the worlds and no more, the other is called interior, and is for the renewing of the *Mo'hin* of *Z'uN*. Similarly, there are two types of guidance for the world: one for its subsistence, and one, which is dependant on the actions of man, for the guidance on the basis of justice, reward and punishment.

---

[143] Of *Abah* and *Imah*
[144] *NHY*
[145] The *Sephirot* on top of *NHY*

Fourth chapter

The construction of the *Partsuf Zeir Anpin*

Introduction

The Partsufim of Zeir Anpin and Nukvah are the root of all the created. It is by them, that the guidance of justice is manifested. The Mo'hin of Z`A are given to him by the Partsufim of Abah and Imah. His construction starts with a first stage of gestation, a second of suckling and a third of growth.

a) *Z'A* integrates the six edges [146] of the world [of *Atsilut*], and *Nukvah* is its *Mal'hut* [147]. *Arikh Anpin* folded his legs [148] and drew them on his *HGT*. The *Kelim* of *Z'A* ascended after them and clothed them [149]. Their shape in *Arikh Anpin*, is the same as their shape in *Z'A*; three on top of three, and *Mal'hut* fourth after them.

Arikh Anpin took them [150], sorted them, and then by his *Zivug* [with his *Nukvah*], took them out. *Abah* and *Imah* took them [151], and repaired them definitely; in three days, forty days, three months and two gestations.

א. ז"א - שש קצותיו של עולם,
ונוק' - מלכות שלו.
קפל אי"א את רגליו והעלם על
חג"ת שלו.
עלו כליו של ז"א אחריהן
והלבישום.
כצורתן באי"א צורתם בז"א –
שלש על גבי שלש,
ומלכות - רביעית אחריהם.

נטלם אי"א ובררם, והוציאם
בזיווגו.
נטלום אוי"א ותקנום לגמרי:
בג' ימים, ובמ' יום, בג' חדשים,
ובג' עיבורים.

---

[146] *Abah* and *Imah* are the *Mo'hin*
[147] Of *Atsilut*
[148] His *NHY*
[149] The *NHY* of *Arich Anpin*
[150] From *NHY* of *Atsilut*
[151] The *Kelim*

Arikh brought up his *NHY* (legs) and the lower third of his *Tiferet,* to clothe his *HGT*; this is called the folding of the legs. This was realized by the returning lights. The *Kelim* of *Z'A* followed and clothed the *Sephirot* of *HGT* and *NHY* of *Arikh* *that* were folded on themselves. By his *Zivug* with his *Nukvah,* *Arikh Anpin* took them out, they were then taken by *Abah* and *Imah* which repaired them completely, by their own *Zivug*[152].

The folding of the legs of *Arikh Anpin* was the first force given to the broken *Kelim* to ascend to *Atsilut*. *Arikh Anpin* is the root of all the *Partsufim* of *Atsilut*; he therefore needs to repair all the *Kelim* so that everything will be attached to him. The first steps of clarifications are in *'Hokhma Stimaah* and in the *Dikna*.

b) In three days, how? Those are the three days of *Klita* (insemination): the first day, *Abah* repaired the right in them [*Z'uN*], the second day, *Imah* repaired the left in them, the third day, *Abah* gave of himself[153] to *Imah* and they were joined [the right and the left side].	‬ב. ג ׳ ימים כיצד ? אלו ג ׳ ימים של קליטה . יום א ׳: תיקן אבא את הימין שבהם. יום ב׳: אימא את השמאל שבהם. יום ג׳: נתן אבא את שלו באימא, ונתחברו אלה באלה.

---

[152] Of *Abah* and *Imah*
[153] Of what he repaired

There are three *Miluim* [154] [of sparks]: The *Miluy* of *MaH* is nineteen, the *Miluy* of *SaG* is thirty seven, and the *Miluy* of *'AV* is forty six.

ג' מילוים הם :

מילויו של מ"ה - יי"ט. ושל ס"ג - לי"ז, ושל ע"ב - מי"ו.

For the *Tikun* of *Z'A*, six of the nineteen [sparks] entered on the first day, six on the second, and seven on the third. Why six [155] ? Because the lines [columns] of *Z'A* are repaired by them. On the third [day], one more because of the joining of the lights [of the right and left columns].

תיקונו של ז"א —

ו' מיי"ט נכנסים ביום ראשון, ו' בב', ז' בג'.

למה ו' ? שקויו של ז"א נתקנים בהם.

ובשלישי אחד יותר מפני חבורם של אורות.

Thirty seven [sparks] in thirty seven days, this makes forty days [156], the infant is formed by the light of *Imah*, forty six [sparks], in forty six days [157], as the three months needed to distinguish the fetus.

לי"ז בלי"ז ימים - הרי מ' יום.

נוצר הולד באורה של אימא, מי"ו במי"ו ימים ; כמשלוש חדשים

—

זמן היכרו של עובר.

---

[154] In the sense of filling. Each name of *ASMB* less the initials of *YKVK* (26)

[155] After it is only one spark a day

[156] With the three first days

[157] This makes a total of 86 days (close to 3 lunar months)

After the *Kelim* ascended, one hundred and two sparks entered. At first, nineteen[158] sparks of the aspect of *MaH* entered; six the first day, six the second, and seven the third day.

The first day, the aspects of the right side of this selection were repaired, corresponding to: *'Hesed, Netsah*, half of *Tiferet*, half of *Yesod* and half of *Mal'hut*, by the *Tipah* (Drop) of *Abah*.

The second day, the aspects of the left side were repaired, corresponding to: *Gevurah, Hod*, half of *Tiferet*, half of *Yesod* and half of *Mal'hut*, by the *Tipah* of *Imah*.

On the third day, *Abah* gave the parts he repaired to *Imah;* the parts merged, became one, and were set in a three-column configuration. Afterwards, thirty seven[159] sparks of the aspect of *SaG,* and forty six[160] sparks of the aspect of *'AV,* came to the *Kelim*.

c) The construction of Z'A [includes]: *Kelim*, sparks, and lights. The *Kelim* that broke, the sparks that descended, and the lights that departed [went back up when the *Kelim* broke]. They came back and	ג. בנינו של ז"א – כלים וניצוצות ואורות: כלים שנשברו, ניצוצות שירדו, אורות שנסתלקו. חוזרים ונתקנים זה בזה בג' עיבורים – של ז' חדשים, ושל ט', ושל י"ב.

---

[158] *MaH* (45) – 26 = 19
[159] *SaG* (63) – 26 = 37
[160] *'AV* (72) – 26 = 46

repaired one another [161] in three gestations [162]; one of seven months [163], one of nine [164], and one of twelve [165] months.

Imah and Tevunah joined as one, and there are three levels of Yesod in them: Yesod of Imah, Yesod of Tevunah, and the place of the cutting when they are separated and cut from each other.

אימא ותבונה מתחברים כאחד, וג' מקומות של יסוד יש בהם: יסודה של אימא, ויסודה של תבונה, ומקום החתך - כשהן מתפרדות נחתכות זו מזו.

His Kelim [166] are repaired by Yesod of Tevunah, his sparks, at the place of the cutting, and his lights, by Yesod of Binah [Imah]. In the lower world, there are also three sections [167].

נתקנים כליו ביסודה של תבונה, ניצוציו במקום החתך, אורותיו ביסודה של בינה. כנגדם למטה ג' מדורות.

A Partsuf includes three components: Kelim, sparks, and lights. At the beginning, in the 'Olam Hanikudim, only six Sephirot

---

[161] By being together, the damage was their separation from each other
[162] One for the sparks, one for the Kelim and one for the lights
[163] For the lights
[164] For the sparks
[165] For the Kelim
[166] Of Z'A
[167] In the woman (Nidah, 31, 1)

of *Z'A* came out; the parts needed for his *HBD* stayed inside of *Imah*. At the time of the breaking of the *Kelim*, the lights went back up[168], the *Kelim* and the sparks descended to *Beriah*. The three need to be repaired, to unite and make the *Partsuf*. The *Tikun* is then to reunite these three aspects again, by the three gestations of seven, nine, and twelve months.

| d) The body of *Z'A* is composed of ten *Sephirot*. Seven *Sephirot* [169] were established in seven month[170], and three[171] in the twenty four month of the suckling; eight month each. Seven [months] which are nine, because *Da'at* divides in *'Hasadim* and *Gevurot*. | ד. גופו של ז״א עשר ספירות. נתבררו ז׳ ספירות בז׳ חדשים, וג׳ ספירות בכ״ד חדשים של יניקה, ח׳ חדשים לאחת. ז׳ שהם ט׳, שהדעת מתחלק לחסדים וגבורות. |

The *Tikun* for the lights was of seven months, for the *Kelim*, twelve months, and for the sparks, nine months. *Hod*, *Yesod* and *Mal'hut* were not repaired during the gestation; they were repaired during the suckling. These three *Sephirot* had to go through the eight[172] higher *Sephirot* (one month for each *Sephira*), which makes the twenty four month of the suckling. Sometimes *Da'at* is not counted, and this makes a total of twenty one month.

---

[168] They first came down to the end of *Atsilut* and then went up
[169] *Keter, 'Hokhma, Binah, 'Hesed, Gevurah, Tiferet, Netsah*
[170] Of the gestation
[171] *Hod, Yesod* and *Mal'hut*
[172] Seven *Sephirot* and *Daat*

e) They are three *Kelim:* *NHY* is the first *Keli*, [the keli of] *HGT* is in his interior, and [the keli of] *HBD* is in the interior of *HGT*.

ה. ג׳ כלים הם: נה״י כלי א׳, פנימי לו חג״ת, פנימי לו חב״ד.

There are three *Neshamot*[173] in them: *Nefesh* in *NHY*, *Rua'h* in *HGT*, and *Neshama* in *HBD*. When are they repaired? During the gestation, the suckling, and [when they receive] the *Mo'hin*[174].

וג׳ נשמות בתוכם — נפש בנה״י, רוח בחג״ת, נשמה בחב״ד. אימתי הם נתקנים ? בעיבור יניקה ומוחין.

The *Kelim* of *HGT* dress inside the *Kelim* of *NHY* and make their interior, but they[175] are exterior to the *Kelim* of *HBD*, which are clothed inside them. In the same way, their lights are clothed in each other.

During the gestation, which is the first selection in the three pillar arrangement, the *Mo'hin* are of the lowest level and are called *NHY* of the *Mo'hin;* they are of the aspect of *Nefesh*.

---

[173] *Nefesh, Rua'h* and *Neshama*
[174] When they are in *Z'A*
[175] *HGT*

During the suckling, the lights grow and the *Mo'hin* are of a higher level and are called *HGT* of the *Mo'hin;* they are of the aspect of *Rua'h*.

During the growth, the *Mo'hin* are fully developed to guide *Z'uN* with the force of *HBD;* they are of the aspect of *Neshama*.

f) *NHY*[176] in the gestation how[177]? Its *NHY*[178] and its *HGT*[179] are its exteriority, *HBD*[180] is the *Nefesh* in them.	ו. כיצד נה"י בעיבור ? נה"י וחג"ת שלו - חיצוניות, וחב"ד - נפש בתוכם.
HGT[181] [is repaired] in the suckling; its *NHY*[182] and its *HGT*[183] are its exteriority, *HBD*[184] is the *Rua'h* in them.	חג"ת ביניקה ? נה"י וחג"ת : חיצוניות, וחב"ד רוח בתוכם.
HBD[185] [is repaired] in the growth, these are all the *HGT* that ascend and	חב"ד בגדלות ? אלו חג"ת שעולים ונעשים חב"ד, ונה"י במקומם,

---

[176] Which is the exterior *Keli*
[177] How is it repaired?
[178] *NHY* of *NHY*
[179] *HGT* of *NHY*
[180] *HBD* of *NHY*
[181] Which is the intermediate *Keli*
[182] *NHY* of *HGT*
[183] *HGT* of *HGT*
[184] *HBD* of *HGT*
[185] Which is the interior *Keli*

become *HBD*, the *NHY* take their place[186], and new *NHY* are renewed lower for them[187].	ונה"יי אחרים מתחדשים להם למטה.
HBD spreads down on all; this corresponds to the *Neshama* [soul] which contains *Nefesh*, *Rua'h*, *Neshama*, *'Hayah* and *Ye'hidah*. *NRN*[188] are the interiority, *'Hayah* and *Ye'hidah* are their encircling, and all the *Kelim* are exteriority to them [*HBD*].	חב"ד יורדים בכולם, זהו נשמה, שבה נרנח"יי. נר"ן - פנימים, ח"יי – מקיפים להם. חזרו כל הכלים חיצוניות לגבה.
Three composed of three[189]: *NHY HGT HBD* in *NHY*, [the three aspects of the exterior *Keli*] *NHY HGT HBD* in *HGT*, [the three aspects of the intermediate *Keli*] *NHY HGT HBD* in *HBD*, [the three aspects of the interior *Keli*]	ג' של ג': נה"יי חג"ת חב"ד - בנה"יי, נה"יי חג"ת חב"ד - בחג"ת, נה"יי חג"ת חב"ד - בחב"ד. ונרי"נ של גדלות בתוך כולם.

---

[186] Of *HGT*

[187] To replace the *NHY* that became *HGT*

[188] *Nefesh*, *Rua'h* and *Neshama*

[189] Each one of the three aspects has its own three aspects

| NRN of the growth, inside of all. | |
| As it is in man: flesh, veins, bones, and NRN in them. | כנגד באדם – בשר וגידים ועצמות, ונר״נ בתוכם. |

The *Kelim* have three levels: Interior, intermediate and exterior. *NHY* is the exterior *Keli* of *Z'A*, *HGT* is the intermediate *Keli*, and *HBD* is the interior *Keli*. For each level, there are three aspects as:

NHY of *NHY* - exterior *Keli* of *NHY*
HGT of *NHY* - middle *Keli* of *NHY*
HBD of *NHY* - interior *Keli* of *NHY*
NHY of *HGT* - exterior *Keli* of *HGT, etc.*

NHY is the aspect of *Nefesh*, *HGT* of *Rua'h,* and *HBD* of *Neshama*. *NHY* of *NHY* is the aspect of *Nefesh* of *NHY*, *HBD* of *HBD* is the aspect of *Neshama* of *HBD*, and so on. All the aspects of *NHY* are repaired during the gestation, the aspects of *HGT* during the suckling, and the aspects of *HBD* during the growth. *HGT* becomes *HBD*, *NHY* becomes *HGT* and new *NHY* are made for *Z'A*.

| g) [During the growth] All the [*Kelim* of the aspects of] *NHY* become *NHY*, all the *HGT* [become] *HGT,* and all the *HBD* [become] *HBD.* HBD of NHY: bones[190], | ז. כל הנה״י נעשים נה״י, וכל חג״ת - חג״ת, וכל חב״ד - חב״ד. חב״ד שמנה״י - עצמות, חב״ד מחג״ת - קרומות, חב״ד מחב״ד - מוחין; שכן בגופו של אדם |

---

[190] Cranium

HBD of *HGT*: veins, *HBD* of *HBD*: *Mo'hin*, As in the body of man[191]: bones, veins, cranium and *Neshama* inside of them.	עצמות קרומות ומוחין, ונשמה בתוכם.
The exteriors are the *NHY* and *HGT*, the interiors are the *HBD*. As for man: Body and soul (*Neshama*).	חזרו כל החיצוניות - נה"י וחג"ת, וכל הפנימיות - חב"ד להם. כנגדם באדם - גוף ונשמה.
The *Kelim* divided as interiors and exteriors; the *Neshama* in them is lights and sparks. From all of these elements, *Z'A* is constructed.	נחלקו הכלים לפנימי וחיצון, ונשמה בתוכם - אורות וניצוצות. בנינו של ז"א משוכלל מכל אלו.

During the growth, all the aspects of *NHY* of the *Kelim* as: *NHY* of *NHY*, *NHY* of *HGT*, and *NHY* of *HBD* become the *NHY* of *Z'A*. All the *HGT* become the *HGT* of *Z'A*, and all the *HBD* become the *HBD* of *Z'A*. The *HBD* of *Z'A* is then of all the interior aspects, *HGT* of the middle aspects, and *NHY* of the exterior aspects. *HGT* and *NHY* are the exteriors aspects of *HBD*, as it is in man, whose body is the exterior aspect, and whose the soul is the interior aspect.

---

[191] In his head: cranium, veins and brains

h) There are four gestations [for Z'A], two for [the making of the levels of] its exteriors [192], and two for [the making of the levels of] its interiors [193] - gestation for its six lower [Sephirot], and gestation for its Mo'hin.

ח. ד' עיבורים הם:
ב' בחיצוניותו, וב' בפנימיותו –
עיבור דו"ק, ועיבור דמוחין.

The first gestation [for its six lower Sephirot] is of twelve months, the second [for its Mo'hin] is of nine [months]; this is for its exteriors. It is the same for its interiors; nine [months for its six lower Sephirot], and seven [months for its Mo'hin].

עיבור ראשון י"ב חדשים, שני לו
ט' בחיצוניות.
כנגדם בפנימיות - של ט', ושל ז'.

Four gestations are necessary for Z'A inside of Imah, in order for him to reach his full growth. Gestation for the interiors of the Mo'hin is seven months, and for the six lower Sephirot; nine months. Gestation for the exteriors of the Mo'hin is nine months and for the six lower Sephirot; twelve months. The firsts gestations are in Tevunah, the seconds are in Imah.

---

[192] NHY and HGT
[193] HBD

i) The [period of the] suckling is twenty four month; [194] it is for the clarification of *Hod, Yesod* and *Mal'hut*. From here to growth, it will take eleven years and one day. How? Seven parts of *NHY* of *Tevunah* [enter *Z'A*] in seven years, and its crown[195]; in one day. From her [196] , come out the revealed *'Hasadim,* from the chest [of *Z'A*] and downward.

They [the *'Hasadim*] come down to group in *Yesod* [of *Z'A*], and return upwards on their columns [*Netsah* and *Hod*], until they ascend in all the six edges [of *Z'A*].

Five *Gevurot* come down afterwards, and are sweetened [appeased] in *Yesod* [of *Z'A*]; two and a half in the descent, the rest

ט. היניקה כ״ד חדשים .
בירורם של הי״מ.
ממנה לגדלות י״א שנה ויום א׳.
כיצד ?
ז׳ פרקיהם של נה״י דתבונה בז׳
שנים,
ועטרה שלה ביום א׳,
שבו יוצאים החסדים מגולים מן
החזה ולמטה.

יורדים ונכללים ביסוד,
וחוזרים בקוויהם מלמטה למעלה
עד שעולים בכל שש קצותיו.

ה׳ גבורות יורדות אחריהן
ונמתקים ביסוד,
ב׳ וחצי בירידה,
והשאר בחזירתם של חסדים
עולים ומתמתקים אתם.

---

[194] Eight months each
[195] Of *Yesod*
[196] The crown of *Yesod*

[are sweetened]; by the *'Hasadim* returning upwards.	
The *'Hasadim* are the growth for *Z'A*, the *Gevurot* are the growth for *Nukvah*. The guidance of the masculine is of the right, the one of the feminine is of the left.	החסדים - גידולו של זעיר. והגבורות - גידולה של נוק׳. שהנהגתו של זכר לימין, ושל נוק׳ לשמאל.

The *Sephirot* that are repaired during the gestation are: *Keter*, *'Hokhma*, *Binah*, the *'Hasadim* and *Gevurot* of *Da'at*, *'Hesed*, *Gevurah*, *Tiferet*, and *Netsah*. Nine *Sephirot* (including *'Hasadim* and *Gevurot* of *Da'at*) are like the nine months of gestation for a newborn.

The ones repaired in the suckling are: *Hod*, *Yesod* and *Mal'hut*, they are repaired latter[197], as a newborn that cannot walk when first born; he needs the sustenance (suckling) to strengthen his legs to stand on them. During the time of the gestation, *Z'A* is not really acting as it is being built, at the time of suckling it starts to act, and at the growth it is ready to act completely.

j) The *'Hasadim* returned[198] to *'Hesed* and *Gevurah* [of *Z'A*], they[199] augmented and	י. חזרו החסדים לחסד ולגבורה, והגדילום, והם נכפלים. נמצאו כל אחד ו׳ שלישים .

---

[197] In 24 months
[198] From *Yesod* of *Z'A*
[199] The *'Hasadim*

doubled[200]. Each one is now of six thirds; three stayed in their place[201], two went up from *'Hesed* to *'Hokhma*, two from *Gevurah* to *Binah*, one third [shared] in each [*'Hesed* and *Gevurah*, went up] on the right and left of *Da'at*.

ג' נשארים במקומם,
ב' מחסד עולים לחכמה,
וב' מגבורה לבינה,
והשלישי שבשניהם לימין ושמאל שבדעת.

Two of the thirds of *Tiferet* doubled and became four, two [stayed] in their place, one ascended to *Keter* of *Nukvah*, one went up to the one that is covered[202], and doubled [in size]. One [covered] remained in his place, and one[203] came up with him[204] until *Keter* [of *Z'A*].

נכפלו ב' שלישיו של ת"ית ונעשו ד'.
ב' למקומם,
א' לכתר נוק',
וא' עולה למכוסה, ומכפילו.
נשאר א' במקומו,
וא' מעלהו עמו עד הכתר.

Two Kings [*Zeir Anpin* and *Nukvah*] are sharing the same crown; *Z'A* completes himself with his.

נמצאו שני מלכים משתמשים בכתר אחד.
וז"א נשלם בשלו.

---

[200] From three thirds to six thirds
[201] In the *Kelim* of *'Hesed* and *Gevurah*
[202] The first third of *Tiferet* which is hidden or covered
[203] Of the uncovered thirds
[204] Covered third

| The ascent of the *Hasadim* to *HBD* is of three years, and one year to *Keter*, which is above them. | עליתם של חסדים בחב״יד ג׳ שנים, ושנה, לכתר ששורה על גביהם. |
| This is the time necessary for the ascent of the *Hasadim* to *Keter*. Thirteen years and one day, this is the period of growth. | יומם של חסדים עולים לכתר. והרי י״ג שנים ויום א׳, זה הגדלות. |

The essential of the guidance proceeds from *Da'at* of *Z'A*. *Da'at* is the outcome of all the *Tikunim* of *'Hokhma* and *Binah* of *Z'A*. For this reason, *Da'at* needs to spread down more than the rest of the *Mo'hin*, because for them[205], standing in three columns in *Z'A*, is sufficient. *Da'at* spreads in all[206] the sides of *Z'A*, and in *Nukvah*.

For the guidance, *Z'A* receives five *'Hasadim* from *Da'at*, and *Nukvah* receives five *Gevurot*[207]. *'Hesed, Gevurah*, and *Tiferet* are composed of three thirds each, the superior third of *Tiferet* is hidden or covered by *Yesod* of *Tevunah*. After the complete spreading of the *'Hasadim* in *Z'A*, and their rise until *Keter*, *Z'A* has attained the growth level.

---

[205] The other *Mo'hin*
[206] Also up to *KHB*
[207] From *Daat* also

k) On top[208] of צ, there are ל מ, which are encircling [Z'A]. The time[209] [for them to arrive] is two years; these are from *Imah*.

יא. למעלה מצ' - ל' מ' מקיפין.
זמנם שתי שנים,
אלו מאימא.

The interior [*Mo'hin*] of *Abah*; [take] three years [to enter in Z'A], and two years for his encircling; this is the completion of the beard.

פנימים דאבא ג' שנים.
וב' שנים למקיפיו,
הרי זה מלוי זקן.

After the entrance of the interior *Mo'hin*, the exterior *Mo'hin* encircle Z'A. There are two distinct *Mo'hin* that come to Z'A, *Mo'hin* of *Imah* that arrive first, and then the *Mo'hin* of *Abah*. The *Mo'hin* that are given from *Abah* and *Imah* to Z'A, do not enter completely in him; only the *NHY* do, the rest stays on top of him, encircling his head.

NHY are composed of nine parts, corresponding to the צ, and spread in the nine *Sephirot* of Z'A. The encircling are ל מ, they do not need to spread in him, and stand on his exterior in the three-column arrangement of kindness, rigor and mercy.

After receiving all the *Mo'hin* from *Abah* and *Imah*, it is the first growth; twenty years have past, Z'A has now a fully grown beard, like a twenty year old man.

---

[208] On top of צ which represents the interior *Mo'hin*, there are *Mo'hin* encircling by the outside
[209] For the exterior *Mo'hin*

l) [When *Z'A* receives its *Mo'hin*] From *Tevunah*, there are states of infancy and growth [for *Z'A*], a first state of infancy, and a first state of growth. Similarly, from *Imah*; there is a second state of infancy, and a second state of growth.	יב. בתבונה - קטנות וגדלות : קטנות ראשונה, וגדלות ראשונה. כנגדם באי׳ - קטנות וגדלות שנייה.
As it is for the first[210], it is for the second[211]. The firsts *Mo'hin* are from lower [*Tevunah*], the seconds are from higher [*Imah*].	כענינו בראשונה ענינו בשנייה. שמוחין הראשונים מלמטה, והשניים מלמעלה.

As there are two gestations, there are two growths; the first is from *Tevunah,* and the second is from *Imah*. The first *Mo'hin* are from *Tevunah* and the seconds, more important, are from *Imah*. It is only after the second growth, that *Z'A* has reached its full potential. This is *Gadlut* 2.

---

[210] The entrance, the propagation (of the *Mo'hin* of *Tevunah*).
[211] The *Mo'hin* from *Imah*

Fifth chapter

The construction of the *Partsuf Nukvah*

Introduction

The Partsuf Nukvah represents the feminine – the principle of receiving. It comprises of two distinct Partsufim: Ra'hel and Leah. Once the Partsuf Zeir Anpin has been constructed, the construction of Nukvah starts, with the lights given to her by Abah, Imah and Zeir Anpin. When she is complete, she separates herself from Z'A, and can now act as an independent Partsuf.

a) The [first] state of *Nukvah* corresponds to one dot, the seventh of six [*Sephirot*]. When *Z'A* ascends, she ascends with him, during the gestation, the suckling and the growth.	**א.** קביעותה של נוקי – נקודה אחת, שביעית לששה. עלה הזייא, ועלתה אחריו בעיבור וביניקה ובגדלות.
b) [During the gestation] The Six edges [of *Z'A*], are three on three [212], and *Mal'hut* is fourth after them on *Yesod* [of *Z'A*].	**ב.** ו״ק תלת גו תלת, והמלכות רביעית אחריהן על היסוד.
[During the suckling] *NHY* [213] descended, and *HGT* [214] were revealed. *Mal'hut* stayed attached to the back of *Tiferet*.	ירדו נה״י ונתגלו חג״ת, נשארה המלכות דבוקה בת״ת מאחוריו.
[During the growth] *HGT* ascended and became *HBD*, *Mal'hut* ascended and was rooted in *Da'at*[215].	עלו חג״ת ונעשו חב״ד, עלתה המלכות ונשרשה בדעת.

---

[212] *NHY* fold on *HGT*

[213] Of *Z'A*

[214] Of *Z'A*

[215] Of *Z'A*

Z'uN grow together; there is perfection for the masculine only when it completes itself with its feminine. Even if they are two distinct *Partsufim* and have their own *Tikunim*, all the time that *Z'A* is being built, *Nukvah* is attached to him.

During the gestation, she is attached to his *Yesod*, [she is still as one dot], during the suckling, she is on his *Tiferet*, and during the growth, she is on his *Da'at*. It is only once his construction is complete that *Z'A* starts to build *Nukvah* by his *NHY*[216].

c) She [*Nukvah*] descends [from *Da'at*] to be constructed; she is built by the rears of his *NHY* [of *Z'A*]. *Tiferet*[217] [of *Z'A*] in *Keter* [of *Nukvah*], *Netsah* and *Hod* [of *Z'A*] in *'Hokhma* and *Binah* [of *Nukvah*], *Yesod* [of *Z'A*] in *Da'at* [of *Nukvah*] between her shoulders, those are the first parts [218] [of *NHY*], the remainder[219] in the rest of her body [of *Nukvah*].	ג. יורדת להבנות – בנינה מנה"י שלו מאחוריהם. ת"ת בכתר, נו"ה בחו"ב, יסוד בדעת שבין כתפיה. אלו פרקים ראשונים, והשאר בשאר גופה.

---

[216] Of *Z'A*

[217] The two lower thirds of *Tiferet*

[218] Of three parts

[219] Of the parts of *NHY*

Eight years for eight parts [220], the masculine *Yesod* [of *Z'A*] is two parts long; he ends at the end of her *Tiferet*[221]. From there, the *Gevurot* descend from him to her *Yesod*[222]; [this is done] in one day.

ח׳ שנים לח׳ פרקיהם,
שיסודו של זכר ארוך ב׳ פרקים.
נמצא כלה בסוף ת״ת שלה,
שמשם יורדות הגבורות ממנו
ליסוד שלה ביום א׳.

They [the *Gevurot*] return upwards [in *Nukvah*] from *Yesod* to *Tiferet;* one year, from it [*Tiferet*] to *Da'at;* one year, one year for [the construction of] her *Keter,* and from *Da'at* to *Keter;* one year. These are [make] the twelve years and one day; because the *Nukvah* precedes the masculine [by one year].

חוזרים מלמטה למעלה :
מיסוד לת״ת שנה א׳,
ממנה לדעת שנה א׳,
שנה אחת לכתר שלה,
מדעת לכתר שנה א׳.
אלו י״ב שנים ויום א׳,
שהנוק׳ מקדמת לזכר.

Z'uN were attached by their backs, about them he says: "Back and front you have restricted me, and laid your hand upon me" (Tehilim 139, 5)

נמצאו דו״נ מדובקים מאחוריהם,
ועליהם הוא אומר (תהלים קלט,
ה):
"אחור וקדם צרתני".

---

[220] Three parts of *Netsah*, three parts of *Hod* and two parts of *Yesod*
[221] Of *Nukvah*
[222] Of *Nukvah*

To become a complete *Partsuf*, *Nukvah* needs to be repaired by *Z'A*. After his growth, once he has received his *Mo'hin*, *Z'A* starts to spread his lights to her by way of his rears, to build her.

She descends from his *Da'at*[223]; his *Tiferet*[224] makes her *Keter*, the different parts of his *NHY* make her *HGT*, *NHY* and *Mal'hut*. In *Da'at* of *Z'A* are rooted the *'Hasadim* and *Gevurot*, the *Gevurot* go down to the *Yesod* of *Z'A*, there, they are softened[225] by the *'Hasadim* that were already there. From *Yesod* of *Z'A*, the *Gevurot* are given to the *Da'at* of *Nukvah*, they go down until her *Yesod* and then ascend to her *Keter*. During all this process, *Nukvah* is attached to the back of *Z'A*.

d) *Imah*[226] comes out from *Z'A*, his *Mo'hin* [227] are contained in her [in *NHY* of *Imah*], and *NHY* of *Abah* are clothed in her [in *NHY* of *Imah*].	ד. יוצאת אימא מז״א, ומוחיו בתוכה. ונה״י אבא מלובשים בה.
They enter [228] to build *Nukvah*, and she is	נכנסים ובונים את הנוק׳ מתוקנת על ידיהם.

---

[223] Of *Z'A*
[224] Of *Z'A*
[225] Term used to express a softening of their harshness
[226] Her *NHY*
[227] Of *Z'A*
[228] In *Nukvah*

appeased [229] by them. *'Hesed* [of *Imah*] spreads in Z'A who pushes out the *Gevurot* from his rears, they are given through them[230] to *Nukvah*, and she separates from him [Z'A].

Nukvah is built from the left[231], and Z'A from the right[232]. They find themselves facing each other, and she is built[233] in front of him.

On them, it is written: "And the rib, which the Lord G-d had taken from man, made He a woman, and brought her to the man" (Bereshit, 2, 22)

וחסד נמשך לז״א שדוחה הגבורות שבאחוריו,
וניתנים על ידיהם לנוק׳,
וננסרה ממנו.

נמצא:
נוק׳ בנויה לשמאל,
וז״א לימין.
חוזרים זה נגד זה ונבנית לפניו.

עליהם הוא אומר (בראשית ב, כב):
"ויבן ה' אלהים את הצלע ויביאה אל האדם".

The *Mo'hin* inside of Z'A are the *NHY* of *Imah*; in them[234] are clothed the *NHY* of *Abah*. During the construction of *Nukvah*,

---

[229] The *Gevurot* given by *Abah* and *Imah* to her are more appeased than the ones given by Z'A
[230] The rears of Z'A
[231] From the aspects of the *Gevurot*
[232] From the aspects of the *'Hasadim*
[233] Being separated from him
[234] *NHY* of *Imah*

they leave[235] from inside *Z'A*, and dress inside *Nukvah* to make her a complete *Partsuf* that is detached from *Z'A*.

Gevurot are given to *Nukvah* directly by *Imah*, and she is more appeased than when she was receiving them from *Z'A*. *'Hesed*, which together with the *Mo'hin* left *Z'A*, is drawn back to him, and *Z'A* pushes out by his rear his *Gevurot* to *Nukvah*.

Nukvah has now *Gevurot* from Abah, *Imah* and *Z'A*, and there is *Nessirah*[236] (she separates from him). The rears of *Nukvah* being complete in the aspects of *Gevurot*, and the ones of *Z'A* in the aspects of *'Hasadim*, they are now face to face.

e) The construction of a *Partsuf* is done by the twenty two letters. Twenty two letters are given from *Z'A* to *Nukvah*; they integrate in her *Yesod*, and [she also receives] מנצפך (the five final letters) corresponding to the *Gevurot* and containing *M'N*[237].	ה. בנינו של פרצוף בכ"ב אותיות. כ"ב אותיות לנוק' מז"א, נכללים ביסודה, ומנצפ"ך גבורות מ"ן בתוכם.
Twenty two more letters are given to her[238] from *Imah*, but not through *Z'A*, and also מנצפך containing *M'N*.	וכי"ב אחרות ניתנות לה מאימא שלא על ידו, ומנצפ"ך מ"ן בתוכם.

---

[235] The *Mo'hin*
[236] Cutting

The twenty two letters [make] one *Dalet* (ד) with an a: ך. They are two *Dalet* [239] with two axis, which make one ם; this is the *Keli*.	כ״ב אותיות דלת וציר נמצאו שתי דלתות ושני צירים שהם ם אחת, זה הכלי.
Twenty two letters from *Imah* are like one [240]; one month for the twenty two letters and five months for the five מנצפך; that makes the six months corresponding to the period between the young girl and puberty.	כ״ב אותיות מאימא נכללים כאחד, חודש לכ״ב אותיות, והי חדשים להי של מנצפ"ך – ששה חדשים שבין נערות לבגרות.

The twenty two letters build the *Partsuf*, and then end in its *Yesod*. For the construction of *Nukvah*; twenty two letters are given to her[241] by Z'A, once they build her, they end in her *Yesod* and make a *Keli*. The five ending[242] letters: מנצפך, are her five *Gevurot,* and also contain the *Mayim Nukvin*. After the *Nessirah*, when *Abah* and *Imah* have built her, they also give her twenty two letters, מנצפך and *Mayim Nukvin*.

---

[237] *Mayim Nukvin*

[238] To *Nukvah*

[239] One from Z'A and one from *Imah*

[240] One letter with the shape of a *Dalet* (ד)

[241] Before the *Nessirah* (separation from Z'A)

[242] Also called double, because they are written differently if they are the end letter

The twenty two letters given by *Z'A* make an axis in a shape of
two ו and one י ; as a ד[243], and likewise from *Abah* and *Imah*,
the two ד complement each other and make a ם, which has a
shape of a *Keli*. With this in place, *Z'uN* are now ready for the
guidance of the world.

f) There is a screen (divider) that separates one world from another. From this screen, the ten *Sephirot* of the lower world come out from the ten *Sephirot* of the higher world. All the worlds are equal[244], but the quintessence of the higher is superior.	ו. ופרגוד בין עולם לעולם, שממנו יוצאין עשר ספירות של תחתון מעשר ספירותיו של עליון. כל העולמות שוים, אלא שכחם של עליונים יפה.
Beriah came out [245] ; the separate beings came to be[246]. The *Neshamot* of the Tsadikim are from *Beriah*, below it, is *Yetsirah;* from there the angels come out, and below it, is *'Asiah;* from there the physical emerges.	יצתה **בריאה**, התחילו הנפרדים. נשמותיהם של צדיקים מבריאה, למטה ממנו **יצירה**, שמשם מלאכים. למטה ממנה **עשיה**, שמשם גשמים.

---

[243] *Gematria* of the three letters = 22
[244] They all contain 10 *Sephirot* and five *Partsufim*
[245] From the world of *Atsilut*
[246] Started to exist

The total of the worlds is four; upon them, the four letters of the Name[247] B'H, govern. י in Atsilut; by it, all the repaired levels are put in order. ה descends from it (Atsilut) to Beriah, and guides it. ו to Yetsirah, and ה to 'Asiah.

כללם של עולמות ד',
שבהם שולטים ד' אותיות של
השם ב״ה.
י' באצילות, שבו כל מדרגותיו
נסדרות בתיקונם.
וה' יורדת ממנו לבריאה,
ומנהיגתה ; **ו' ליצירה** ; **ה' לעשיה.**

In parallel (to these four worlds) there are in this world: דומם, (mineral), צומח (vegetal), חי (animal), and מדבר (man), As it is written:
"Every one who is called by My Name; for I have created him for My glory, I have formed him; yes, I have made him" (Isaiah, 43, 7)

כנגדם בעולם - דצח״ם.
וכן הוא אומר (ישעיה מג, ז) :
"כל הנקרא בשמי ולכבודי
בראתיו יצרתיו אף עשיתיו".

The lights of Mal'hut of Atsilut collided, and made a divider was put between Atsilut and Beriah. From there, other Partsufim similar to the ones in Atsilut, were formed in the lower worlds; but of a lower force, since the lights were dimmed by the divider.

---

[247] Tetragamon (יקוק)

Because of the diminution of the light's intensity, existence for separated entities became possible. Under the divider of *Atsilut*, is the world of *Beriah* - the world of the *Neshamot*. Under the divider of *Beriah*, is the world of *Yetsirah* - the world of the angels. Under the divider of *Yetsirah*, is the world of *'Asiah* - the physical world.

Atsilut is of the aspect of *Abah*, *Beriah* of *Imah*, *Yetsirah* of *Z'A,* and *'Asiah* of *Nukvah.* In parallel to these four worlds [ABYA], there are four types of existence in our world; mineral corresponding to *'Asiah*, vegetal corresponding to *Yetsirah,* animal corresponding to *Beriah,* and man corresponding to *Atsilut.*

Sixth chapter

The *Zivugim* of *Zeir Anpin* and *Nukvah*

Introduction

For the abundance to come down to the world, Zeir Anpin needs to unite with Nukvah. There can be abundance only when the masculine and the feminine are in harmony. Each day, according to the actions of man, the Tefilot during the week, Shabbat or holydays, and depending on time, various configurations allow different Zivugim, and therefore outflows of abundance of variable intensities.

a) The abundance of the world proceeds from the *Zivug* of *Z'uN*. There are five *Zivugim:* *Israel* and *Ra'hel,* *Ya'acov* and *Ra'hel,* *Israel* and *Leah,* *Ya'acov* and *Leah* from the chest up, *Ya'acov* and *Leah* from the chest down.	א. שפעו של עולם מזיווגם של זו״ן. ה׳ זיווגים הם . ישראל ורחל, יעקב ורחל, ישראל ולאה, יעקב ולאה מן החזה ולמעלה, יעקב ולאה אף מן החזה ולמטה.

All the abundance that comes down to the world, proceeds from the various *Zivugim* of *Z'uN*. The one of *Israel* and *Ra'hel* is of the highest level. *Israel* represents all of *Z'A*, *Ra'hel* is the essential of *Nukvah*. The abundance that is bestowed by this *Zivug* is the most complete. The other *Zivugim* of *Z'uN* are of different levels, in various times, and of lesser plenitude.

Each new day, is of a new emanation that governs it. For each day, there are new *Zivugim* of different aspects of *Z'uN*. A full day is divided in two; day and night, and each half is again divided in two[248]. For each part, there is a *Tefilah*, for the two parts of day: *Sharhrit* and *Minha,* for the two parts of nights: *Arvit* and *Tikun Hatsot*.

---

[248] Dawn and day, dusk and night

Generally[249], the *Zivugim* are:

Shahrit - Ya'acov and *Ra'hel*
Minha – Israel and *Leah*
Arvit – Ya'acov and *Leah* (from the chest up)
Tikun Hatsot – Ya'acov and *Leah* (from the chest down)
The *Zivug* of *Israel* and *Ra'hel* is realized during the *Tefilah* of *Mousaf* on Shabbat and some holydays, and on other special occasions.

b) *M'D*[250] and *M'N*[251], are the essential of the *Zivug*. *M'N* proceeds from the feminine, and *M'D* from the masculine. There is no *M'D* without *M'N*, and there is no *M'N* without desire. As it is written: "And your desire shall be to your husband" (Bereshit, 3, 16).	ב. מ״ד ומ״ן – זה גופו של זיווג. מ״ן מן הנקבה ומ״ד מן הזכר. אין מ״ד בלא מ״ן. ואין מ״ן בלא תשוקה. הוא שהכתוב אומר (בראשית ג, טו): "ואל אישך תשוקתך".

The masculine corresponds to *'Hesed* and *MaH*, the feminine to *Gevurah* and *BaN*. As explained above, the *Tikun* is only possible by the *Zivug* [union] of the masculine and the feminine. There are two conditions needed for the *Zivug* to be possible: the *Partsufim* have to be constructed, and the

---

[249] There are some variations
[250] *Mayim Duchrin* (masculine waters)
[251] *Mayim Nukvin* (feminine waters)

feminine has to stimulate a reaction from the masculine. This stimulation happens when she brings up her *Mayim Nukvin* (of the aspect of *BaN*), which then provokes the descent of the *Mayim Duchrin* from the masculine (of the aspect of *MaH*).

The masculine reacts, stimulated by the feminine, which is in turn motivated by the actions of the Tsadikim. In addition, because of the *Tikunim* realized by men with the *Tefilot* and the *Mitsvot*, *Nukvah* brings up her *Mayim Nukvin*, and in response; *Mayim Duchrin* come down for the completion of the *Zivug*.

c) [For the *Tikun*] *Nukvah* includes her ramifications[252] in her, and adorns herself with her ornaments[253]. All the worlds, *Beriah*, *Yetsirah* and *'Asiah* are the *Tikun*[254] of *Nukvah*. She motivates *Z'A*, to attach and unite with her by a first and a second union.	ג. נכללת נוקבא בענפיה, ומתקשטת בקישוטיה. כל העולמות בי״ע - תיקוניה של נוק׳. מתעוררת לז״א להתחבר עמו, ומזדווג עמה – ביאה ראשונה וביאה שניה.

From *Nukvah* all the lower worlds spread down, each one according to its individual functions. The angels accomplish the divine will, and men serve the Lord by their free choice. When all these worlds will completely attach to her, she will be ready for the ultimate *Zivug*. This attachment in the "ideal

---

[252] The worlds of *Beriah*, *Yetsirah* and *'Asiah*

[253] The *Hechalot*

[254] She is complete only when her branches (ramifications) attach to her

mode" will only be accomplished at the end of times. However, there are now *Zivugim* of *Z'uN* everyday, but which only integrate partially the worlds of *Beriah*, *Yetsirah* and *'Asiah*.

d) On the first union, it is said: "A woman is an unfinished vessel, and binds a covenant only with who makes her a *Keli*." (Sanhedrin 22.b).	ד. ביאה ראשונה – זהו שאמרו (סנהדרין כב:) : "האשה גולם היא ואינה כורתת ברית אלא למי
He [*Z'A*] puts *Rua'h* in her [*Nukvah*]; this corresponds to Benyamin – *BaN*, by him [255], she brings up her children [256] ; these correspond to the *Neshamot* of the Tsadikim. Lights illuminate from her [*Nukvah*] for the guidance of the worlds; they are the lights of *BaN*.	שעשאה כלי". נותן רוח בתוכה, זה בנימין - ב"ן, שבו מעלה בניה למעלה – אלו נשמותיהן של צדיקים. ואורות מאירים ממנה להנהגתו של עולם, אלו אורות של ב"ן.
All the outcomes of *BaN* depend on her [*Nukvah*]; from her 613 limbs she draws them [257], the renewal	כל תולדותיו של ב"ן תלוים בה, ומתרי"ג איבריה היא ממשיכתם, מחידושו של א"ס ב"ה שהוא מחדש בהם,

---

[255] *BaN*
[256] The *Neshamot* that fell during the breaking of the *Kelim*
[257] The renewal of the lights of *BaN*
[258] The renewal of the lights of *MaH*

[of the lights] is from the *Ein Sof B'H*, who regenerates [their strength] in them [by a special emanation]; these are the *M'N*.

אלו מ"ן.

In the second union; *M'D* come down to their level [of *M'N*] from the *Yesod* of the masculine; these corresponding to the lights of *MaH*, and all the outcomes of *MaH* depend on him [*Z'A*]. From his 613 limbs he draws them[258], the renewal [of the lights] is from the *Ein Sof B'H*, who regenerates [their strength] in them [by a special emanation].

ביאה שניה –
יורדים כנגדן מ"ד מיסודו של
זכר ;
אלו אורות של מ"ה,
וכל תולדותיו של מ"ה תלוים בו.
מתרי"ג איבריו הוא ממשיכם,
מחידושו של א"ס שהוא מחדש
בהם.

All [*M'N* and *M'D*] descend to her *Yesod* [of *Nukvah*], remain there for the time of the gestation, come out and spread[259] in all the worlds.

יורד הכל ביסודה, ויושב שם זמן
עיבורו.
יוצא ומתחלק לכל העולמות.

---

[259] The abundance

The *Nukvah* cannot receive from *Z'A*, until she becomes a *Keli;* this is the goal of the first union. The *Keli* will be realized by the two ז that make the ם, as explained above. The *Neshamot* of *Israel*[260] are the *M'N* for *Z'uN*, and *Z'uN* are the *M'N* for *Abah* and *Imah*. The abundance first comes to *Z'A*, then to *Nukvah,* and from her, to the lower worlds.

| e) *MaH* and *BaN* are the foundation of all the created[261]. By them[262], are manifested the actions of the *Ein Sof*, *B'H* [the Emanator] [263], and the receivers [264]. They [265] are renewed by the *Zivug* of *Z'uN;* *MaH* from the masculine, and *BaN* from the feminine. | ה. מ״ה וב״ן - בנינם של כל הנבראים. שבהם נראים מעשיו של א״ס ב״ה במשפיע ומקבל, מתחדשים בזיווגם של זו״נ. מ״ה מן הזכר, וב״ן מן הנקבה. |

There is no existence that is not composed of the aspects of *MaH* or *BaN:* the influencer and the receiver, the masculine and the feminine etc. The *Ein Sof*, *B'H* influences when there is instigation from the receiver, the latter corresponding to the aspect of *BaN*. This influence is transmitted by different illuminations of the aspect of *MaH*, and then by *Nukvah*, after

---

[260] Their *Mitsvot* and *Tefilot*
[261] Everything is composed of both (*MaH* and *BaN*)
[262] *MaH* and *BaN*
[263] His emanation are of the aspect of *MaH*
[264] The receivers are of the aspect of *BaN*
[265] *MaH* and *BaN*

her *Zivug* with *Z'A*. From *Z'A,* is the renewal of the aspect of *MaH*, and from *Nukvah;* the renewal of the aspect of *BaN*.

f) There are two unions for the *Zivug*: the kissing [266], and the *Yesodot* [267]. The kissing is in the heads, their *Zivug* is double; the *Rua'h* of the masculine is in the mouth of the feminine, and the *Rua'h* of the feminine is in the mouth of the masculine. There are then two *Ruhot* unified as one. The *Zivug* of the *Yesodot* is done after the union [of the kisses]; the masculine bestows to the feminine, and the feminine [bestows] to the world.	ו. ב׳ חיבורים לזיווג - נשיקין ויסודות. נשיקין בראש, זיווגם כפול – רוחו של זכר בפיה של נקבה ורוחה של נקבה בפיו של זכר. נמצאו שתי רוחות מתחברים כאחד. זיווגם של יסודות, אחר שנתחברו, משפיע הזכר לנקבה והנקבה לעולם.

There are two steps for the *Zivug*, the first is realized in the heads of the *Partsufim;* it is the kissing (the *Zivug* of the mouths); by them the interiors of both *Partsufim* attach, this attachment is afterwards extended to the rest of the *Partsuf*. The second, is the *Zivug* of the *Yesodot*, it is from this *Zivug* that emanations are spread to the worlds.

---

[266] To attach the interiority of the masculine with the one of the feminine
[267] To attach the exteriority of the masculine with the one of the feminine

Seventh chapter

The clothing of the *Partsufim*

Introduction

Each world: Atsilut, Beriah, Yetsirah and 'Asiah, consists of five main Partsufim. These Partsufim are clothed in one another; the higher inside the lower. Depending on the state and growth of Z'A, his Mo'hin could come from different Partsufim. When Z'A receives his Mo'hin directly from Abah and Imah, he is fully grown, and can now influence with all his strength.

a) The sum of the *Partsufim* is twelve [268], the rest [269] ; emanates from them [They are] :

Arikh Anpin and his *Nukvah*, *Abah* and *Imah*, the first *ISOT* [*Israel Sabbah*, *Tevunah*], the second *ISOT* [*Israel Sabbah2*, *Tevunah2*], *Israel*, *Ra'hel*, *Ya'acov* and *Leah*. They are clothed one inside the other[270].

א. כללם של פרצופים י״ב,
והשאר מתפשטים מהם :
א״א ונוקביה, או״א,
יסס״ת ראשונים, יסס״ת שניים,
ישראל ורחל, יעקב ולאה,
מתלבשים אלו בתוך אלו.

b) The innermost [*Partsuf*] of these[271], is *Arikh Anpin* and his *Nukvah*, they make one *Partsuf;* the masculine on the right, and the feminine on the left.

ב. פנימים מכולם - א״א ונוקביה,
פרצוף אחד הם,
שהזכר בימין והנקבה בשמאל.

Abah and *Imah* are on his arms [272] ; *Abah* is on the right, and *Imah* on the left. There are three parts of the

ועל זרועותיו –
אבא לימין אי״י לשמאל.
ג׳ פרקין בזרוע :
הראשון בחב״ד, השני בחג״ת,

---

[268] Beside the *Partsuf* of *Atik*
[269] Other lights that are not complete *Partsufim*. (See Chap. 7, e.)
[270] The superior *Partsuf* is clothed inside the lower to guide him
[271] *Partsufim*
[272] Of *Arich Anpin*

arm: the first [part] is in their *HBD* [of *Abah* and *Imah*], the second is in their *HGT*, the third is in their *NHY*. Their *Keter* [of *Abah* and *Imah*] are in [273] his throat [*Binah* of *Arikh Anpin*], and they[274] extend downward his navel[275]. His body[276] is covered by them [*Abah* and *Imah*] the navel; one half by *Abah*, and one half by *Imah*.

השלישי בנה"י.
וכתרם בגרונו.
ומגיעים עד טבורו.
נמצא גופו עד הטבור מכוסה
תחתיהן,
חציו מאבא וחציו מאימא

c) *ISOT* [start] from the chests of *Abah* and *Imah* and extend downward. Their *Keter* are in the chests [of *Abah* and *Imah*], the rest of their bodies [of *ISOT*] are in the parts of *NHY* [of *Abah* and *Imah*].

ג. יסו"ת מחזיהם של או"א
ולמטה.
כתרם בחזה, ושאך כל גופם
בפרקיהם של נה"י.

From their chests [of *ISOT*], *ISOT* 2 follow in the same

מחזה שלהם יסו"ת שניים כסדר
הזה.

---

[273] At the level of his throat

[274] *Abah* and *Imah*

[275] Of *Arich Anpin* (until the second third of *Tiferet*, which corresponds to the navel)

[276] Of *Arich Anpin*

[277] Until the first third of *Tiferet* and not the second, as above Because new *NHY* are given to them when the first *NHY* become *Mo'hin* for *Z'A*

arrangement. *Abah* and *Imah* extend downward until the chest[277] of *Arikh Anpin,* and *ISOT* extend downward until his navel [of *Arikh Anpin*].	נמצאו: אוי״א כלים בחזה של אי״א, ויסוי״ת בטבורו.
When they [*NHY* of *ISOT*] enter *Z'A,* they elongate their legs [*NHY*] inside him, and reach together with him until the [lower] extremity of the world [of *Atsilut*].	כשבאים בזי״א - מתארכים רגליהם בתוכו. ומגיעים עמו עד סוף העולם

A *Partsuf* is composed of one *Sephira,* or of a few *Sephirot* acting in coordination. A *Partsuf* is constantly interrelating with the other *Partsufim.* Sometimes a *Sephira* acts as one of ten *Sephirot* of a 'Olam, sometimes it acts individually or with others, as a *Partsuf.* Each *Sephira* subdivides in ten *Sephirot,* as for *Keter* there are: *Keter* of *Keter,* '*Hokhma* of *Keter,* and so on until *Mal'hut* of *Keter.* Each one of these ten *Sephirot* is also a configuration of ten *Sephirot,* as for example: *Keter* of *Keter* of *Keter,* or '*Hokhma* of *Keter* of *Keter,* and these again divide in ten. Therefore, a *Partsuf* is a configuration of ten *Sephirot,* each one in turn containing a certain number of *Sephirot.*

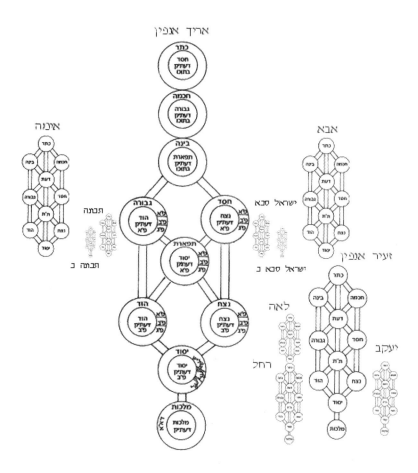

There are five main *Partsufim:*

- *Arikh Anpin*
- *Abah*
- *Imah*
- *Zeir Anpin*
- *Nukvah*

And one on top of them: *'Atik Yomin* [clothed inside *Arikh Anpin*].

From these five *Partsufim*; emerge seven more. They emanate from the ten *Sephirot* as follows:

From *Keter:*   - *'Atik Yomin* and his *Nukvah*
                - *Arikh Anpin* and his *Nukvah*

From *'Hokhma:* - *Abah*
                - From *Mal'hut* of *Abah* - *Israel Saba**
                - From *Mal'hut* of *Israel Saba* - *Israel Saba* 2

From *Binah:*   - *Imah*
                - From *Mal'hut* of *Binah* -*Tevunah**
                - From *Mal'hut* of *Tevunah* - *Tevunah* 2
Israel Saba and *Tevunah* are also called by their initials *ISOT* or *ISOT* 2.

From *'Hesed, Gevurah, Tiferet, Netsah, Hod, and Yesod:*
                Zeir Anpin also called **Israel**
                From *Zeir Anpin* - **Ya'acov**

From *Mal'hut*:- Nukvah, divided in two *Partsufim:*
                Ra'hel and Leah

Each *Partsuf* is clothed inside another, the higher in the lower. We will see here the position of the *Partsufim* in *Atsilut;* their positions and interactions are similar in the worlds of *Beriah*, *Yetsirah* and *'Asiah*.

The $G'aR^{278}$ of *'Atik Yomin*^{279} are in the superior world [above *Atsilut*], his $Z'aT^{280}$ are inside the ten *Sephirot* of *Arikh Anpin*. *Arikh Anpin* reaches from the top to the bottom of *Atsilut*.

Abah and *Imah* dress his right and left arm, their *Keter* reach his *Binah*^{281}, and their *Mal'hut* his *Tiferet*^{282}. *ISOT* dresses NHY^{283} of *Abah* and *Imah*, *ISOT* 2 dresses the *NHY* of *ISOT*.

Tiferet and *NHY* of *Israel Saba* 2 dress inside *Tiferet* and *NHY* of *Tevunah* 2, and then into *Z'A*. *Tiferet* dresses in *Keter*^{284}, the first part of *NHY* of ISOT2 in *'Hokhma, Binah* and *Da'at*^{285}, the second part of *NHY* in *'Hesed, Gevurah* and *Tiferet*^{286}, and the third part of *NHY* in *Netsah, Hod* and *Yesod*^{287}. The masculine *Yesod* of *Israel Saba* is longer than the feminine

---

[278] The three first *Sephirot*. His *G'aR* are called "*Radl'a*" (the unknown head)

[279] *Atik* Yomin is the *Mal'hut* of the world above

[280] Seven lower *Sephirot*

[281] *Arich Anpin* is different from the other *Partsufim*, his *Binah* is under *Keter* and *'Hokhma* which are in a straight line

[282] Until the second part of *Tiferet* which is divided in three

[283] *Netsah, Hod* and *Yesod*. More precisely from the end of the first part of *Tiferet* and *NHY*

[284] Of *Z'A*

[285] Of *Z'A*

[286] Of *Z'A*

[287] Of *Z'A*

Yesod of *Tevunah;* he reaches lower than her *Yesod*[288], and ends in *Tiferet* of *Z'A*.

Depending on his growth, *Z'A* dresses *NHY* of ISOT2, *NHY* of *ISOT*, or *NHY* of *Abah* and *Imah*. When the *NHY* of the higher *Partsuf* is clothed inside the lower *Partsuf*, it is given to the higher *Partsuf* new *NHY* to be complete again. The new *NHY* given to *ISOT* surround the head of *Z'A*, and then spread down on the exterior of his backside until his *Tiferet*, similar to the shape of a ל.

d) *Z'A* [starts] from the chests of *ISOT*, and extends down. They[289] dress inside one another, and then into him [*Z'A*].	ד. ז״א מחזיהם של יסו״ת ולמטה, מתלבשים זה בזה, ומתלבשים בתוכו.
Ra'hel [starts] from his chest [of *Z'A*] and extends down, she is sometimes back to back, and sometimes face to face [with *Z'A*]. The *Yesod* of the feminine is one and-a- half parts [long], the one of the masculine is two parts [long].	ורחל מחזה שלו ולמטה, פעמים אב״א ופעמים פב״פ. יסוד של נקבות פרק וחצי, ושל זכרים שני פרקים.
The *Yesod* of *Abah* emerges from the *Yesod* of *Imah*,	נמצא יסודו של אבא יוצא מיסוד אי׳

---

[288] Of *Tevunah*
[289] *Israel Saba* in *Tevunah*

inside of *Z'A*, from the chest[290] until the *Yesod* [of *Z'A*].

בתוכו של ז״א מן החזה עד היסוד,

It is from him [from an illumination of *Yesod* of *Abah*], that *Ya'acov* comes out from the chest of *Z'A* and lower, in front of him. The face of *Z'A,* to the back of *Ya'acov*, sometimes he [*Ya'acov*] comes to his side, his face [of *Ya'acov*] in front of *Ra'hel*. These are the rears [*NHY*] of *Abah*, which make a *Partsuf* [*Ya'acov*], from the lights of his *Yesod* [of *Abah*].

שממנו יוצא יעקב מחזהו של ז״א

ולמטה לפניו,

פני ז״א באחוריו של יעקב ;

ופעמים שהוא בא לצדו, פניו בפני

רחל.

אלו אחוריים של אבא שנעשים

פרצוף באור יסודו.

The rears [*NHY*] of *Imah*, [extend] from the chest of *Z'A* upwards. They[291] make a *Partsuf* with the lights of her *Yesod* [of *Imah*] - this is *Leah;* [she starts] from *Da'at* [of *Z'A*, and extends] until his chest, [she is] in the back of *Z'A*, her face to his back.

אחוריים של אי׳ מן החזה של ז״א

ולמעלה

נעשים פרצוף באור יסודה - זו

לאה,

מן הדעת עד החזה, מאחוריו של

ז״א, פניה באחוריו

---

[290] *Tiferet* of *Z'A*
[291] *NHY* of *Imah*

It is from an emanation of the longer *Yesod* of *Israel Saba,* inside *Z'A,* that *Ya'acov* comes out. His *Keter*[292] is at the level of *Tiferet* of *Z'A,* and he extends until *Mal'hut* [of *Z'A*].

From an emanation of the *Yesod* of *Tevunah,* inside of *Z'A,* *Leah* comes out. Her *Keter*[293] is at the level of his *Da'at*[294], and extends down to his *Tiferet*[295]. From the same emanation, *Ra'hel* comes out, her *Keter* is at the level of his *Tiferet*[296], and her *Mal'hut* is at the level of the *Mal'hut* of *Ya'acov.*

There is a notion of closeness and interaction, depending on whether the *Partsufim* face or turn their back to each other. The three possibilities are: face to face, face to back, or back to back. Face to face is the ideal level, and corresponds to the bestowing of abundance, while back to back is the lower level, and corresponds to dissimulation and rigor.

Sometimes, *Ra'hel* is back to back with *Z'A* from his chest down, and *Ya'acov* has his back to the face of *Z'A.* She could also be face to face with *Z'A,* who is in the middle, having her and *Ya'acov* on his sides - the three of them looking at each other. Sometimes, *Leah* is face to back with *Z'A,* and when *Ra'hel* is also there, the legs of *Leah* stand on her head[297].

---

[292] Of *Ya'acov*
[293] Of *Leah*
[294] Of *Z'A*
[295] Of *Z'A*
[296] Of *Z'A*
[297] Of *Ra'hel*

When *Ra'hel* is ready for the *Zivug*, she comes face to face with *Z'A,* and takes the place of *Ya'acov,* which takes the place of *Essav.* There are many other possibilities of interrelations between these *Partsufim*, each one inciting its own effects and particular influence.

The guidance of the world is dependent on the different positioning and interaction, of these masculine and feminine *Partsufim*, since they have a direct effect on the measure and balance of the factors of kindness, rigor and mercy.

e) At the back of *Ya'acov,* between him and *Z'A,* there is *Leah D'hM* [298] [דור המדבר], which is his *Nukvah.*	ה. מאחוריו של יעקב בינו ובין ז"א –לאה דור המדבר, נוק' שלו.
From the two sides of *Z'A,* [there are] two diagonal lights: *"The Clouds of Glory"* on his right, and *"The Manna"* on his left.	מב' צדדיו של ז"א שני אורות באלכסון – עניני כבוד לימינו, ומן לשמאלו.
From the two sides of *Leah D'hM,* [there are] two lights: *"The Scepter of*	מב' צדדיה של לאה דור המדבר – שני אורות : מטה האלהים, ומטה משה.

---

[298] *Partsuf Leah*
[299] The mixed multitude
[300] As described above

Elokim", and *"The Scepter of Moshe"*.	
From the two sides of *Ya'acov*, [there are] two lights: *"Erev Rav"*[299] on his right, and *"Essav"* on his left. Three lines of three and three, when *Ra'hel* is back to back, they are standing this way[300].	ומב׳ צדדיו של יעקב – שני אורות : ערב רב לימינו, ועשו לשמאלו. נמצאו ג׳ שורות של ג׳ ג׳. כשרחל אבי״א עומדים כסדר הזה.

These other lights, or *Partsufim*, are not considered as complete *Partsufim*; their actions are temporary and at particular times only.

f) [There are] Eighteen [aspects of] *Leah;* they are from the Malhuts of *Abah* and *Imah*. How? *Mal'hut* of *Abah* is in its place[301], *Mal'hut* of *Imah* is on its outside[302], these make two [aspects]. *Mal'hut* of *Abah* emerges outward from the *Mal'hut*	ו. יי״ח לאה הם ממלכיותיהם של אוי״א. כיצד ? מלכות אבא במקומה ומלכות אימא חוצה לה , הרי ב׳ . מלכותו של אבא בוקע מלכותה של אי׳י

---

[301] In *Mal'hut* of *Imah*
[302] Of *Mal'hut* of *Abah*
[303] The other aspects of *Leah*

of *Imah* and illuminates outside of her, these make three [aspects].

Mal'hut of *Imah* emerges outward, trough the body of *Z'A*, and illuminates outside of him, these make four [aspects].

The most important of all [the *Leah*], is the one on the outside, the rest [303] are subordinate to her.

ומאירה חוצה לה,

הרי ג'.

מלכותה של אי' בוקעת ויוצאה,

בוקעת גופו של ז"א ומאירה חוצה לו,

הרי ד'.

עיקר שבכולם זו שבחוץ,

והשאר טפלות לה.

g) The four *Mo'hin* of growth, and the four of infancy [of *Z'A*]; make eight [aspects of *Leah*, that come from the Malhuts of *Abah* and *Imah*, during the infancy and growth of *Z'A*].

The ones [*Mo'hin*] of growth start to enter, the ones of infancy have not yet finish to exit, these are eight more [aspects of *Leah*].

Two more [aspects of *Leah*] add to them; one of infancy and one of growth, because of the multiplication of the lights.

Those are the eighteen wives allowed to the king..

ז. ד' מוחין דגדלות

וד' מוחין דקטנות,

הרי ח'.

התחילו של גדלות ליכנס,

ולא גמרו של קטנות לצאת,

הרי ח' אחרות.

ושתים אחרות נוספות עליהם –

א' מקטנות וא' מגדלות,

מפני ריבוים של אורות.

אלו י"ח נשים שהמלך מותר בהם.

Leah has different aspects: First, *Yesod* of *Abah* brings out one *Leah*, *Yesod* of *Imah* also brings one out, then the *Yesod* of *Abah* breaks out from the *Yesod* of *Imah* and brings out a *Leah* outside; all this is still inside of *Z'A*. *Yesod* of *Imah* then spurts out again, but this time outside of *Z'A*, and makes the main *Leah*.

h) Higher than all the *Partsufim*, is *'Atik*, it is the *Mal'hut* of *Adam Kadmon*, which became *'Atik* in *Atsilut*. Similarly in *Beriah*, for *Mal'hut* of *Atsilut* [304], and in *Yetsirah* [305], and 'Asiah[306].	ח. למעלה מן הפרצופים - עתיק, זו מלכותו של א"ק שנעשית עתיק באצילות. כנגד זה בבריאה - ממלכותה של אצילות; וכן יצירה, וכן עשיה.
'Atik is masculine and feminine; masculine in his front, and feminine in his back. The [three] first [*Sephirot*] of *Nukvah* [of *'Atik*] are higher than *Atsilut*, this is the *Radl'a*[307].	עתיק - דכר ונוקבא, זכר בפניו ונוק' באחוריו. ראשונות של נוק' למעלה מאצילות, זו רדל"א.

---

[304] Becomes *Atik* in *Beriah*
[305] *Mal'hut* of *Beriah* becomes *Atik* in *Yetsirah*
[306] *Mal'hut* of *Yetsirah* becomes *Atik* in *'Asiah*
[307] The Unknown Head

The [seven] lower *Sephirot*[308] dress in *Arikh Anpin:*	תחתונות שבה מתלבשים באי״א :
'Hesed [of *'Atik*] in *Keter* [of *Arikh Anpin*],	חסד בכתר,
Gevurah in *'Hokhma,*	גבורה בחכמה,
Tiferet in *Binah,*	ת״ת בבינה,
the first parts of *NHY* [of *'Atik*] in *HGT,*	פרקים ראשונים של נה״י בחג״ת,
the second [parts of *NHY*] in *NHY,*	ושניים בנה״י,
the third [parts] of *Netsah* and *Hod,* together with *Mal'hut* [of *'Atik*], in *Mal'hut* [of *Arikh Anpin*].	ושלישים שבנו״ה ומלכות עמהם - במלכות.
[From there] They come out and illuminate all the other worlds.	יוצאים ומאירים בכל שאר העולמות.

'Atik is superior to all the *Partsufim.* It is realized by the *Mal'hut* of *Adam Kadmon*.It has ten *Sephirot*, his front corresponding to his masculine aspect, and his back corresponding to his feminine aspect (his *Nukvah).* His masculine aspect is not clothed inside *Atsilut.* The first three *Sephirot* of his *Nukvah* are above *Atsilut,* and make together the *Radl'a* - רישה דלא אתידע (the unknown head).

The seven lower *Sephirot* dress inside *Arikh Anpin* in the following manner: *'Hesed* in *Keter, Gevurah* in *'Hokhma,*

---

[308] Of *Nukvah* of *Atik*

Tiferet in *Binah*, the first part of *NHY* in *'Hesed, Gevurah* and *Tiferet*, the second part of *NHY* in *Netsah, Hod and Yesod*, the third part of NH[309], and *Mal'hut* of *'Atik* in *Mal'hut* of *Arikh Anpin*.

It is the same in the three other worlds of *Beriah, Yetsirah* and *'Asiah,* the only difference being that the *Mal'hut* of the world above becomes the *Partsuf 'Atik* of the world below.

---

[309] *Yesod* has only two parts

Eighth chapter

The *Tikunim* of the *Partsufim* and the worlds

Introduction

The Tikunim of the Partsufim are the actions and inter-relations of the Partsufim, and their influence for the guidance of the worlds. First, are the Tikunim of Arikh Anpin, and then the ones of Zeir Anpin and Nukvah. These Tikunim are from the head, or the face of the Partsufim. Each world is made of Partsufim, Levush (garments of the Partsufim), encircling lights, and Hechalot.

a) [There are] Three heads in 'Atika[310] [Arikh Anpin]; Radl'a[311], Gulgolta and Mo'ha[312]. Two that make three[313]: Gulgolta, Avirah and Mo'ha; the Da'at of 'Atik is hidden in Avirah. By these[314], all the worlds are directed with kindness, rigor and mercy.	א. תלת רישין בעתיקא : רישא דלא אתידע, גלגלתא, ומוחא. ב' נעשים ג' : גלגלתא אוירא ומוחא ; דעתו של עתיק גנוז באוירא. באלו מתנהגים כל העולמות בחסד בדין וברחמים.

In Hebrew, the word "Tikun" has different meanings. Until now we have associated it with reparation or rectification, but it can also be understood as function, relation or action. Here, the "Tikun" is a description of the actions, illuminations and inter-relations of the Sephirot and Partsufim. These Tikunim will result in various illuminations of different intensities, for the guidance of the worlds.

In Arikh Anpin, are clothed the seven lower Sephirot of the Nukvah of 'Atik Yomin. The first three Sephirot: Keter, 'Hokhma and Binah did not dress inside Arikh, and remained on top of his head; they (KHB of Nukvah of 'Atik) make the

---

[310] In the two Adarot of Rabbi Shimon Bar Yohai, Arich Anpin is called Atika

[311] The unknown head

[312] In the first Atsilut

[313] In the second Atsilut

[314] The three heads

Radl'a – the unknown head; it is called this way because we can not grasp any understanding of it.

The first *Tikun* is the one of the three heads of *Arikh Anpin*:

1- *Gulgolta* - *Keter* of *Arikh Anpin*

2- *Avirah* - In the space between *Keter* and *'Hokhma* of *Arikh Anpin,* there is *Da'at* of *'Atik*

3- *Mo'ha* - *'Hokhma* of *Arikh Anpin*

These three heads are the roots of the three directions of kindness, rigor and mercy. They emanate from *Arikh Anpin* to *Abah* and *Imah,* and from there, to the *Mo'hin* of *Z'A.*

b) The interiority of the heads [315] : הוי״ה, the exteriority : אהי״ה. The first ones[316] [are of the aspect] of ע״ב and his אהי״ה, the seconds [317] [are of the aspect] of ס״ג, the thirds [318] [arc of the aspect] of מ״ה.	ב. פנימיותן של רישין - הוי״ה, החצוניות - אהי״ה. הראשונים דע״ב ואהי״ה שלו, השניים דס״ג, השלישיים דמ״ה.
For each [head] there are [three levels of lights]: Interior, encircling [*Makif*],	פנימי ומקיף ומקיף דמקיף בכל אחת ואחת.

---

[315] Is of the aspect of הוי״ה

[316] In the first head ; *Gulgolta* - *Keter*

[317] In the second head ; *Avirah*

[318] In the third head; *Mo'ha* - *'Hokhma*

and encircling of the encircling [*Makif* of *Makif*].

They differentiate by their *Nekudot*[319].

The first letters have the vowels as pronounced – interiority

The *Miluy*[320] has vowels as pronounced – encircling

The *Miluy* has *Kamatz* as a vowel, and the first letters have vowels as pronounced – encircling of encircling. This is the first head. [*Gulgolta*]

במה הם מתפרשים ?
- בניקודיהם.
מנוקד הפשוט בתנועותיו - זה פנימי ;
מנוקד המלוי, כפשוטו - זה המקיף ;
מנוקד המלוי כולו קמץ, והפשוט בתנועותיו –
זה מקיף דמקיף,
זה הראש הראשון.

The first letters have the vowels as pronounced, and *Segol* instead of *Tsere*.

The *Miluy* has vowels as pronounced.

The *Miluy* has *Kamatz* as a vowel. This is the second head. [*Avirah*]

מנוקד הפשוט בתנועותיו, מקום צירי סגול ;
מנוקד המלוי כפשוטו.
מנוקד המלוי כולו קמץ –
זה הראש השני.

The first letters have the vowels as pronounced, *Segol* instead of *Tsere* and

מנוקד הפשוט בתנועותיו,
מקום צירי סגול ומקום קמץ פתח ;

---

[319] Vowels

[320] Letters that are added for the spelling of each individual letter

Patah instead of *Kamatz*. The *Miluy* has vowels as pronounced The *Miluy* has *Patah* as a vowel. This is the third head. [*Mo'ha Stimaah*]	מנוקד המלוי כפשוטו ; מנוקד המלוי כולו פתח – זה הראש השלישי .

In each one of the three heads, there are aspects of interiority and exteriority, as in all the lights. Each aspect[321] subdivides in three more aspects: Interiority, encircling, and encircling of encircling.

The names of הוי״ה correspond to the aspect of interiority, the names of אהי״ה correspond to the aspect of exteriority. In each head, there are three הוי״ה, and three אהי״ה, the distinction for each one (of the הוי״ה and אהי״ה) is in the *Nekudim* it receives.

c) [There are] Seven *Tikunim* of the head [of *Arikh Anpin*], that are revealed from the seven [lower *Sephirot*] of '*Atik*, their indication is: ג״ט קר״ע פ״ח	ג. שבעה תיקוני רישא משבעה של עתיק, סימנם : ג״ט קר״ע פ״ח.
From '*Hesed* of '*Atik* גולגלתא לבנה - (*Gulgolta Levanah*) of Arikh	גולגלתא לבנה . מחסדו של עתיק. טלא דבדולחא מגבורה שלו.

---

[321] Interiority and exteriority
[322] Of *Netsah* and *Hod*

From his *Gevurah* - טלא דבדולחא (*Tela Debadul'ha*) of Arikh	קרומא דאוירא . מת״ת שלו.
From his *Tiferet* - קרומא דאוירא (*Kroma Deavirah*) of Arikh	רעוא דמצחא - מיסוד שלו.
From his *Yesod* - רעוא דמצחא (*Ra'ava Demits'ha*) of Arikh	
From the first parts of *Netsah* and *Hod* that are higher than *Yesod* - עמר נקי (*'Amer Naki*) of Arikh	עמר נקי מראשיתם של נו״ה, שהם גבוהים מן היסוד.
From their last parts[322] – פקיחו דעינין (*Peki'hu De'inin*) of Arikh	פקיחו דעיינין מסופם.
From *Mal'hut* – חותמא, (*'Hotmah*)	חוטמא - ממלכות.
Leah and *Ra'hel* – שני נחירים (*Shene Ne'hirim*) of Arikh	ב׳ נחירים - לאה ורחל.

The second *Tikun* is of the head of *Arikh Anpin*. It is achieved by the passing of the seven lower *Sephirot* of '*Atik* into the head of *Arikh Anpin,* before they are clothed in him.

- The first *Tikun* - גולגלתא לבנה (*Gulgolta Levanah*) is realized by '*Hesed* of '*Atik*; this is the root of all the '*Hasadim*.

- The second *Tikun* - טלא דבדולחא (*Tela Debadul'ha*) is realized by *Gevurah* of '*Atik* in '*Hokhma Stimaah*. It includes kindness and rigor; kindness because it is on the right column, rigor; because of *Gevurah* of '*Atik*, which is the root of all the *Gevurot*.

- The third *Tikun* - קרומא דאוירא (*Kroma Deavirah*) is realized by *Tiferet* of '*Atik*; it has two actions:
To cover '*Hokhma Stimaah* (of *Arikh*), so that the illumination of *Da'at* of '*Atik* will not be too strong, and for its illumination (of '*Hokhma Stimaah*) when spreading down, not to be too overwhelming for the lower beings.

- The fourth *Tikun* - רעוא דמצחא (*Ra'ava Demits'ha*) is realized by *Yesod* of '*Atik*; his '*Hasadim* shine from the forehead of *Arikh Anpin*. When it is fully revealed, all the rigors are annulled.

- The fifth *Tikun* - עמר נקי ('*Amer Naki*) is realized by the first parts of *Netsah* and *Hod* , which are positioned higher than *Yesod;* it shapes the hair that spreads out from '*Hokhma Stimaah*.

- The sixth *Tikun* - פקיחו דעינין (*Peki'hu De'inin*) is realized by the parts of *Netsah* and *Hod* which are positioned lower than *Yesod*. This *Tikun* is acheived by the eyes, there, the '*Hasadim* are multiplied and always open so as to influence constantly.

- The seventh *Tikun* – חותמא ('*Hotmah*), is realized by the *Mal'hut* of '*Atik;* like the *Mal'hut*, which divides in two, it also splits in two:
- שני נחירים - (*Shene Ne'hirin*), corresponding to the two parts of *Nukvah* – *Ra'hel* and *Leah*.

d) The [other] *Tikunim* of *Arikh Anpin*: נימין[325], חיורתי[324], דיקנא[323] (*Dikna, 'Hivarti, Nimin*) [There are] Three הוי״ה in each head [of *Arikh Anpin*], and one [326] that contains them.

Three הוי״ה, [make a total of] twelve letters, plus the one [327] containing them, make thirteen.

Thirteen חיורתי (*'Hivarti*), from the three [הוי״ה], in *Keter*, their place is between the thirteen נימין (*Nimin*); between each נימא (*Nima*).

Thirteen נימין (*Nimin*); from the three [הוי״ה], in *Avirah*.

Thirteen *Tikunim* of דיקנא

ד. תיקוניו של א״א :
נימין, חיורתי, ודיקנא.
שלש הויות בכל ראש
ואחת כוללת אותם.

שלש הויות י״ב אותיות,
ואחת שקוללתן, הרי י״ג.

י״ג חיורתי - משלש שבכתר,
מקומם בין י״ג נימין, בין נימא
לנימא.

י״ג נימין משלש שבאוירא.

י״ג תיקוני דיקנא משלש

---

[323] The beard
[324] The white on the scalp between the hair
[325] The extremities of the hairs on the head
[326] One more הוי״ה in each head, which contains the three others
[327] The extra הוי״ה is counted as one letter only

(*Dikna*), from the three [הוי״ה], in *'Hokhma*.

שבחכמה.

There are more *Tikunim* of *Arikh Anpin*:

From his *Keter* - חיורתי (*'Hivarti*)

From *Avirah* (*Da'at* of *'Atik*; between *Keter* and *'Hokhma*) - נימין (*Nimin*)

From his *'Hokhma* called *'Hokhma Stimaah* - דיקנא (*Dikna*)

חיורתי (*'Hivarti*), נימין (*Nimin*) and דיקנא (*Dikna*) are called hair and beard, because they spread out in individual conduits.

In each head there are three הוי״ה, each one has four letters, which makes a total of twelve, and one הוי״ה containing all, but counting only as one letter, for a total of thirteen.

From *Keter,* thirteen חיורתי (*'Hivarti*), they are the white parts between each hair. They are four on the right side, four on the left, four on the back, and one containing all. The four on the back, spread down to the *Dikna* of *Z'A*.

From *Avirah*[328]; thirteen נימין (*Nimin*) are divided to spread out the lights of *'Hokhma Stimaah;* they are his hair, also four on the right side, four on the left, four on the back of the neck, and one in the middle of the head containing all. These hairs are white, although hair represents rigor, here there is no rigor. This is the difference with the hair of *Z'A*, which is black and intermingled; while here, they are white and separated.

---

[328] In other writings, they come out from *'Hokhma Stimaah*

The hairs contain the lights of *'Hokhma Stimaah,* and spread them down from its extremities.

e) [There are] Thirteen *Tikunim* of **דיקנא** (*Dikna*) [of *Arikh Anpin*]: **אל רחום ..** **מי אל כמוך. . נושא עון...**	ה. י"ג תיקוני דיקנא : אל רחום וכו' ; מי אל כמוך נושא עון וכו'.
First Tikun: - The two Peot[329]	תיקון א' : ב' פאות.
Second Tikun: - The hair on the upper lip	תיקון ב' : שערות שבשפה עליונה.
Third Tikun: - The vacant space under the nose	תיקון ג' : אורח תחות חוטמא.
Fourth Tikun: - The hair on the lower lip	תיקון ד' : שבשפה התחתונה.
Fifth Tikun: - The space under the mouth	תיקון ה' : אורח תחות פומא.
Sixth Tikun: - The width of the beard	תיקון ו' : רחבה של זקן.
Seventh Tikun: - The two upper sides of the cheeks	תיקון ז' : שני תפוחים שנפנו.
Eighth Tikun: - [The beard on] The upper	תיקון ח' : שטח עליון - מזל נוצר.

---

[329] Hair on each side of the face
[330] Where there is the head of *Z'A*

chin (*Mazal Notser*) *Ninth Tikun*: - The hair between the upper and lower chin *Tenth Tikun*: - The hair on the throat *Eleventh Tikun*: - They are all equal *Twelfth Tikun*: - The free mouth *Thirteen Tikun*: - [The beard under] The lower chin (*Mazal Nake*) The length of the *Mazalot* is until the navel[330].	ט׳ : שערות שבין מזל למזל. תיקון תיקון י׳ : שערות הגרון . תיקון י״א : שכולם שוין. תיקון י״ב : פה פנוי. תיקון י״ג : שטח תחתון – מזל ונקה. שיעורם של מזלות עד הטבור.

There are also hairs [lights] that come out from the face of *'Hokhma Stimaah,* and spread downward. They divide in thirteen, and are called the thirteen *Tikunim* of the *Dikna* of *Arikh Anpin.*

The other *Tikunim* are lights needed for the attainment and abundance. However, the guidance itself is from the *Dikna,* it is through it that the abundance flows. The hairs of the *Dikna* are short and stiff, being of the aspect of rigor. They are also divided in two aspects: Masculine; which includes the first twelve *Tikunim,* and feminine, which comprise the thirteen *Tikun.* Each one of these *Tikunim* has its particular function or action for the general guidance.

The *Dikna* reveals the guidance of kindness, rigor and mercy, which was concealed in *'Hokhma Stimaah,* by bringing it down to *Z'A* [by the two *Mazalot: Notser* and *Nake*].

The *Dikna* will have a supreme function at the end of times:
To reveal the *Yihud*[331] – the divine sovereignty.

f) The *Tikunim* of *Z'A*:	ו. תיקוניו של ז״א : צל״ם.
צל''מ .	צ׳ . מוחין פנימים,
צ – interior *Mo'hin*,	ל׳ מ׳ - מקיפין שבו.
מ, ל – encircling *Mo'hin*.	שבשעה שיצאו היו ד׳, זה מ׳ שלו.
When they came out, they were four [332] ; this corresponds to the מ.	
[They became] Three [333] when they returned in the *Keli* of *Imah;* this corresponds to the ל, and nine [334] [*Mo'hin*] were realized inside of him; this corresponds to the צ.	חזרו שלשה בכליה של אי׳, זה ל׳.
	וט׳ נעשו בגופו, זה צ׳.
The four[335]; are from *KHBD* of *Imah* [336] , the three are from *HGT*[337], and the nine are from *NHY*[338] .	של ד׳ בכחב״ד דאימא, של ג׳ בחג״ת, של ט׳ בנה״י.

---

[331] The unity
[332] 'Hokhma and Binah, 'Hasadim and Gevurot
[333] 'Hokhma and Binah, 'Hasadim and Gevurot became one
[334] The NHY of Tevunah spread in him in nine aspects
[335] The first four Mo'hin
[336] This will make his second encircling Mo'hin
[337] This will make his encircling Mo'hin
[338] This will make his interior Mo'hin

There are two *Tikunim* of *Z'A*; the first *Tikun* is in his *Mo'hin*, and is called his צלמ. His *Mo'hin* are given to him by *Abah* and *Imah*, at first, there are four: *'Hokhma*, *Binah*, *'Hasadim* and *Gevurot*. When entering their *NHY*,[339] they become three; the *'Hasadim* and *Gevurot* joining in *Yesod*.[340]

After entering *Z'A*, *NHY* spread inside of him in nine aspects; this corresponds to the צ, *HGT* make his first encircling; this corresponds to the ל, *KHBD* make his second encircling; this corresponds to the מ.

g) From *Z'A* there are: נימין [341], חיורתי [342], דיקנא [343] (*Nimin, 'Hivarti, Dikna*) From *Arikh Anpin*, they are thirteen [*Tikunim*]. From *Z'A*, they are nine [*Tikunim*]. When his *Tikun* [of *Z'A*] is complete, they become thirteen.	ז. נימין חיורתי ודיקנא בז״א. של א״א - י״ג, של ז״א - ט'. כשנשלם תיקונו נשלמים לי״ג.

The second *Tikun* of *Z'A* is expressed by the lights that come out of him, as the hair on his head, and on his face. These *Tikunim* are similar to the ones of *Arikh Anpin*, but with some differences. From *Arikh Anpin* all the hair come out from

---

[339] Of *Abah* and *Imah*
[340] Of *Abah* and *Imah*
[341] The extremities of the hairs on the head
[342] The white on the scalp between the hair
[343] The beard

'Hokhma Stimaah, from *Z'A*; they come out from his *HBD*. The hairs of *Z'A* are black and intermingled; being more of the aspect of *Gevurah*, the hairs of *Arikh Anpin* are white, and express bounty.

The *Tikunim* of the *Dikna* of *Z'A*, are similar to the ones of *Arikh Anpin*, even if they are nine. However, with an illumination from *Arikh Anpin*, they become thirteen, and act as a principle of kindness for the guidance of justice.

h) From the forehead of *Z'A*, emerge and spurt out from the four *Mo'hin*[344]; the four parashiot of the *Tefilin*. Their garments are their compartments.	ח. במצחו של ז״א בוקעים ויוצאים מד׳ מוחין ד׳ פרשיות של תפילין, ומלבושיהם - בתים שלהם.
They are ten *Sephirot*[345]: *HBD* are the *Tefilin*[346], *'Hesed* and *Gevurah* are the straps of the head, *Tiferet* is the knot on the back; it is from there, that *Leah* comes out. The two straps that come down are *Netsah* and *Hod*; *Netsah* until the chest, and	עשר ספירות הם : חב״ד בתפילין . חו״ג ברצועות של הראש . ת״ת בקשר מלאחריהם, שמשם יוצאת לאה ; ב׳ רצועות יורדות - נו״ה, נצח עד החזה, והוד עד הטבור. תפילין מאימא : קדש, והיה כי יביאך, שמע, והיה אם שמוע.

---

[344] *'Hokhma, Binah,* and *Daat* which is divided in two; *'Hasadim* and *Gevurot*

[345] From the encircling *Mo'hin* – The *Tefilin* of the head

[346] Of the head

Hod until the navel. In the *Tefilin* from *Imah*: קדש, והיה כי יבאך, שמע, והיה אם שמוע In the *Tefilin* from *Abah*: קדש, והיה כי יביאך, והיה אם שמוע, שמע	תפילין מאבא : קדש, והיה כי יביאך, והיה אם שמוע, שמע.

Two more lights come out of Z'A: The *Tefilin* and the *Talit*. The *Tefilin* are the lights of the *Mo'hin* that break out from inside of him, through his forehead. Four[347] that became three inside of him, become four again; these are the four parashiot. Each one of the four lights also brings out an aspect of *Levush* (garment); these are the compartments for the parashiot.

The *Mo'hin* comprise ten *Sephirot*. Therefore, ten lights come out. Since there are *Mo'hin* from *Abah,* and *Mo'hin* from *Imah*, there are two types of *Tefilin:*
Tefilin of *Imah* – *Rashi*
Tefilin of *Abah* – *Rabenu Tam*.

The difference is in the order of the *Parashiot*:

Tefilin of *Rashi*:
1 - 'Hokhma – קדש
2 - Binah - והיה כי יביאך
3 - 'Hasadim – שמע
4 - Gevurot - והיה אם שמוע

---

[347] The *'Hasadim* and *Gevurot* join in *Yesod*

Tefilin of *Rabenu Tam*:

1 - 'Hokhma – קדש

2 - Binah - והיה כי יביאך

3 - Gevurot - והיה אם שמוע

4 - 'Hasadim – שמע

i) A light from *Imah* encircles *Z'A*; this is the white *Talit*.	**ט.** ואור מאימא מקיפו לז״א,
	זהו טלית לבנה - שערות של ז״א,
The hair of *Z'A* appears after his growth ministered by *Imah;* when her new *NHY*[348] are extending on his rear [349] and reach his thorax [350] . They [the lights [351]] are encircling around *Z'A*, and encircling on the head of *Nukvah*.	אחר גדלותו ששרתה עליו אימא, והגיעו נה״י שלה חדשים מאחוריו עד החזה, מקיף לז״א ומקיף על ראש נוקבא.
Encircling of *Z'A* – his *Talit* Encircling of *Nukvah* – his *Tsitsit*.	מקיפו של ז״א - טלית, מקיפה של נוקבא - ציצית שבו.

When *Z'A* is in the growth stage, the *NHY* of *Imah* come down on his back; this makes his hair[352] come out from his head, and

---

[348] Of *Imah*

[349] Of *Z'A*

[350] Of *Z'A*

[351] His hair

[352] Of *Z'A*

go downward until his chest. When they are at the level of his thorax; it corresponds to the *Talit*, when they are at the level of Ra'hel; it corresponds to the *Tsitsiot*.

| j) The *Tikunim* of *Nukvah*[353] are:

Fifteen נימין (*Nimin*) on her head [354] ; their color is purple.

Six *Tikunim* on her face, from the six *Tikunim* of the *Dikna* [of *Z'A*]. When they are complete, they are nine [*Tikunim*]. | י. תיקוניה של נוק׳ –
ט״ו נימין בראשה, וצבעם ארגמ״ן.
וששה תיקונים בפניה מששה
תיקוני דיקנא.
כשהם נשלמים נעשים ט׳. |

The *Nukvah* of *Z'A* is *Ra'hel*; she also has hair on her head, but of a different order and quantity. The six illuminations of her face are parallel to the *Dikna* of *Z'A*, but she has no hair on her face.

| k) Her *Tefilin* [of the head of *Ra'hel*] are on the hand of *Z'A*, they bind on his left, as it is said:
"Set me as a seal upon your heart, as a seal upon your arm" (Shir Hashirim, 8, 6) | יא. תפילין שלה - של יד לז״א,
שהם נקשרים בשמאל שלו,
שנאמר (שיר השירים ח, ו) :
"שימני כחותם על לבך כחותם
על זרועך". |

---

[353] *Ra'hel*
[354] From there, the hair comes out

They [the *Mo'hin* of *Nukvah*] are built by *Netsah* and *Hod* of *Z'A*, in them,[355] are *'Hokhma* and *Binah* of *Imah,* and *'Hokhma* and *Binah* of *Abah*[356].	ומנו״ה דז״א הם נעשים, שבהם חו״ב מאימא וחו״ב מאבא.
The ones of *Abah* make her [*Mo'hin* of] *'Hokhma* and *Binah*. The ones of *Imah* make her [*Mo'hin* of] *'Hasadim* and *Gevurot*, they[357] end in one single compartment [358] , because *Netsah* and *Hod* make two parts of one single body.	של אבא נעשים לה לחו״ב, ושל אימא נעשים לה לחו״ג, נכללים בבית אחד, שנו״ה פלגי גופא

The *Nukvah* [*Ra'hel*] also has an aspect of *Tefilin,* and attaches on the left arm (*Gevurah*) of Z'A.

She (*Nukvah*) has four *Parashiot* in her *Tefilin,* and receives her *Mo'hin* through *Netsah* and *Hod* of *Z'A*:

- *'Hokhma* and *Binah;* from *'Hokhma* and *Binah* of *Abah.*

- *'Hasadim* and *Gevurot;* from *'Hokhma* and *Binah* of *Imah.*

---

[355] *Netsah* and *Hod*

[356] *Abah* and *Imah* make the *Mo'hin* of *'Hokhma* in *Netsah* of *Z'A,* and the *Mo'hin* of *Binah* in *Hod* of *Z'A*

[357] The four *Parashiot*

[358] The *Tefilin* of the hand

l) *Yesod* of *Abah* is preponderant between his own *Netsah* and *Hod*; he stands in *Yesod* of *Imah,* and is preponderant between her *Netsah* and *Hod*. Therefore, there are four lights in him[359], and from them emerge the *Tefilin* on the forehead of *Ya'acov*[360].

יב. יסוד אבא מכריע בין נו״ה שלו,
עומד ביסוד אימא ומכריע בין נו״ה שלה ;
נמצאו בו ד' אורות שמהם תפילין במצחו של יעקב.

These[361] and these[362] come out from *Ya'acov,* and make the *Tefilin* on his forehead. They[363] return to the back, and tie a knot behind him. They[364] return, and emerge [through *Ya'acov*], and then by the forehead of *Ra'hel* to make the *Tefilin* on her head[365].

אלו ואלו יוצאים ביעקב ונעשים תפילין במצחו.
חוזרים לאחוריהם וקושרים קשר מאחוריו.
חוזרים ויוצאים,
עד שיוצאים במצחה של רחל, נעשים תפילין בראשה.

---

[359] *Yesod* of *Abah*
[360] *Tefilin* on the arm of *Rabenu Tam*
[361] The four lights in *Yesod* of *Abah*
[362] The lights of *Netsah* and *Hod* of *Z'A*
[363] The lights in *Yesod* of *Abah* – *Or Hozer* (returning lights)
[364] The lights of *Netsah* and *Hod* of *Z'A* - *Or Hozer* (returning lights)
[365] Of *Ra'hel*

The ones [366] of *Yesod* of
Abah remain in *Ya'acov*, the
ones of *Netsah* and *Hod* of
Z'A remain for *Ra'hel;*
they [367] return to the back,
and tie a knot behind her
[*Ra'hel*].
[The order of the Parashiot]
Of *Ra'hel:* קדש, והיה כי
יביאך, שמע, והיה אם שמוע
[The order of the Parashiot]
Of *Ya'acov:* the two והיה,
follow.

The *Yesod* of *Z'A* is
between the shoulders of
Ra'hel; this is the י *(Yud)*
[knot] of the (arm's) *Tefilin.*
A strap comes out from
it [368], to build the *Nukvah.*
Three wrappings on the
biceps; corresponding to the
three first (*Sephirot*) [*G'aR*
of *Nukvah*]
Seven on the forearm;
corresponding to the seven
lower (*Sephirot*) [*Z'aT* of
Nukvah]

של יסוד אבא נשארים ביעקב.
של נו״ה דז״א נשארים לרחל.
חוזרים לאחור וקושרים קשר
באחוריה.
של רחל : קדש, והיה כי יביאך,
שמע, והיה אם שמוע.
של יעקב : הויות להדדי.

יסודו של ז״א בין כתפיה של רחל,
זה יו״ד שבתפילין.
ורצועה יוצאה ממנה לבנינה של
נוק׳.

ג׳ כריכות בקיבורת - ג״ר,
ז׳ בזרוע : ז״ת,
ג׳ באצבע . נה״י שבמוחיה.

---

[366] Lights
[367] The lights of *Netsah* and *Hod* of *Z'A*
[368] From the *Yud*

> Three on the finger;
> corresponding to the *NHY*
> [of *Z'A*] in her *Mo'hin*.

At first, the four lights in *Yesod* of *Abah* come out with the four lights in *Netsah* and *Hod* of *Z'A*. They go to *Ya'acov;* the lights of *Abah* make his *Mo'hin* – his *Tefilin*, and from him[369] the lights of *Z'A* go to *Ra'hel,* who is behind him, to become her *Mo'hin* - her *Tefilin*. *Ya'acov* corresponds to the *Tefilin* of *Rabenu Tam, Ra'hel* to the *Tefilin* of *Rashi.*

On the hand, the order of the parashiot is the same as in the *Tefilin* of the head, but in only one parchment. The *Yesod* of *Z'A* makes the ׳ *(Yud)* on the *Tefilin* of *Ra'hel,* and from there (the arm of *Z'A*), the building of *Nukvah* starts.

m) A world comprise *Adam* [*Partsuf*], his garment, his encircling, and his *Hechalot.*	יג. כללו של עולם : אדם, ולבושו, מקיפיו, והיכלו.
Adam[370] how? This is the *Tikun* [the structure] of the *Partsuf* – 248 limbs and 365 veins, *NRN* within him, and *'Hayah* and *Ye'hidah* encircling on him.	אדם כיצד ? זה תיקונו של פרצופו . רמ״ח איברים ושס״ה גידים. נר״ן בתוכו, ח״י מקיפים עליו.

---

369 *Ya'acov*

370 The *Partsuf* is named *Adam* (man). Like the body of man, which has 613 members, a *Partsuf* has 613 lights

The light descended to enter in him [371] ; a part entered, and a part remained outside, because the *Keli*[372] was not able to contain it. It encircled his *Keli,* and encircled what was under it [373] . [Linear encircling lights]

ירד האור ליכנס בתוכו, חלק נכנס, וחלק נשאר בחוץ, שאין הכלי יכול להגבילו, מקיף לכליו, ומקיף לכל מה שתחתיו.

From what entered [of the lights], it [374] returned upward, came out, and only encircled its own *Keli*[375] . [Returning encircling lights]

וממה שנכנס - חוזר ויוצא לחוץ ומקיף על כליו בלבד.

There are then two types of encircling lights:
Linear [of the aspect of *Ye'hidah*], and returning [of the aspect of *'Hayah*].

אלו שני מקיפים : ישר וחוזר.

Until now, we have seen the *Tikunim* realized by the interior lights of the *Partsufim*, now we will see the *Tikunim* or actions achieved by the lights on the exterior of the *Partsuf,* as the

---

[371] *Sephira* or *Partsuf*
[372] Of the *Sephira* or *Partsuf*
[373] The lower *Sephirot*
[374] Some parts of lights
[375] Of the *Sephira*

ones realized by his garment, his encircling lights, and the *Hechalot*.

Each world (*ABYA*) is built from these four aspects; *Adam* (*Partsuf* made to the image of man), *Levush* (garment), *Or Makif* (encircling lights), and *Hechalot*.

A *Partsuf* comprise of 613 main forces or lights, which afterward divide into many parts. Correspondingly, man who is as the image of the higher lights, has 248 limbs and 365 veins. This structure is also similar in the Torah, which has 248 positive and 365 negative commandments.

When the light entered the *Keli*, it did not enter completely, because the *Keli* could not contain it. A part of the light remained on the outside, encircling it, and some of the light that had entered came out and encircled the *Keli*.

There are then two types of encircling lights: linear and returning. The linear light, which did not enter in the *Keli*, encircles its *Sephira* and all those under it. The returning light, which entered and came out from the *Keli*, only encircles its *Sephira*. Therefore, each *Sephira* has one interior and two encircling lights.

| n) His *Levush* how [is it realized]? From the striking [of the interior lights of the *Partsuf*] against each other, a *Levush* was made, which | יד. לבושו כיצד ? מהכאותיהם של אורות נעשה לבוש עליהם מבחוץ. |

covers them [376] on the outside[377].	
There is *Hashma'l*[378] from *Imah* for *Z'uN*, when her *NHY*[379] entered in him [*Z'A*], her skin, flesh, bones and veins[380] included with his[381]. With the exception of [some of] her skin[382] that remained in surplus outside, and covers him because of the eyes of the exteriority[383].	וחשמ״ל יש לזו״ן מאימא, שבשעה שנכנסו נה״י שלה בתוכו – עור ובשר ועצמות וגידין נכללו שלה בשלו, חוץ מן העור שנמצא עודף על שלו מבחוץ, ומכסה עליו מפני עיניהם של חיצונים .

The *Levush* is made by the striking of all the interior lights against each other, and is called the exterior of the *Partsuf*.

The difference between the *Levush* and the encircling light is that the encircling light sustains the *Keli*, while the *Levush* is like a curtain that protects him from the exterior lights[384].

Another *Levush* is made for *Z'uN,* from the exteriors of *NHY* [*Tevunah*] of *Imah*. In *NHY* there are three aspects of *Kelim*:

---

[376] For each *Partsuf*
[377] Of the *Partsuf*
[378] Name of the *Levush*
[379] Of *Imah*
[380] Of *Imah*
[381] Skin, flesh, bones and veins
[382] Of *Imah*
[383] The external force – *Sitra A'hra*
[384] Of the *Sitra A'hra*

flesh, bones and veins, and one more aspect of *Keli* from *Mal'hut*[385], which is the skin in surplus of Imah. This last aspect is not clothed in *Z'A,* but rather stands on the outside to envelop him.

This *Levush* of *Z'uN* [*Hashma'l*] clothes him all the way down, and makes a curtain between *Atsilut* and *Beriah.*

o) The *Hechalot* are to a *Partsuf,* as a house is to a man. The Malhuts[386] of the *Sephirot* [are] their exteriority [387] ; [they are] their *Hechalot.* The image of man [the nine superior *Sephirot*], is their interiority.	טו. היכלות לפרצוף כבתים לאדם. מלכויותיהם של ספירות - חיצוניות שלהם, אלו ההיכלות. ודמות אדם – פנימיות בתוכם.
These are not the only types [of aspects] of interiority and exteriority; there are others[388]. However, this is the structure in each world; the lights subdivide among themselves [in interiority and exteriority aspects].	לא שאין פנימיות וחיצוניות אלא זה, אלא שזהו חילוקו של עולם. חוזרים ומתחלקים כל אחד בשלו.

---

[385] Of *Imah*

[386] The *Mal'hut* of each *Sephira*

[387] Of the *Sephirot* or the *Partsufim*

[388] It is not only the *Malhuts* that are exteriorities; there are many other aspects that also divide in interiority and exteriority

p) There are seven Hechalot: [in Beriah]	**טז. ז' היכלות הם** :
First - לבנת הספיר (Livnat Hasapir)	לבנת הספיר,
Second - עצם השמים (Etsem Hashamayim)	עצם השמים,
Third – נוגה (Nogah)	נוגה,
Fourth – זכות (Zehut)	זכות,
Fifth – אהבה (Ahavah)	אהבה,
Sixth – רצון (Ratson)	רצון,
Seventh - קדש קדשים (Kodesh Kodashim)	ק"ק.
[Corresponding to:] First Hechal - Yesod and Mal'hut	היכל יסוד ומלכות : אחד.
Second Hechal - Hod	היכל הוד - אחד
Third Hechal - Netsah	היכל נצח - אחד.
Fourth Hechal - Gevurah	היכל גבורה - אחד.
Fifth Hechal	היכל חסד - אחד.

---

[389] Throne of glory - (Kiseh Hakavod)
[390] Kodesh Kodashim - (קדש קדשים)

- 'Hesed Sixth Hechal - Tiferet Seventh Hechal - The three first [Sephirot]	היכל ת״ת - אחד. היכל ג׳ ראשונות - אחד.
These are the seven Hechalot in Beriah, in them; the Kavod [glory] of the Makom[389] spreads out. Each [Hechal] has Nefesh and Rua'h, and the Kavod is their Neshama in the seventh Hechal[390].	אלו ז׳ היכלות שבבריאה, שבהם כבודו של מקום מתפשט בתוכם. נפש ורוח לכל אחד, והכבוד נשמה להם בהיכל השביעי.
There are three functions [for the Hechalot]: - Separate beings attach to their root. - The Tsadikim enjoy the presence of the Shekhina. - The angels receive from [through] them their tasks.	וג׳ דברים משמשים : נקשרים בהם התחתונים בשרשם, ונהנים הצדיקים מזיו השכינה, ומלאכי השרת מקבלים מהם פעולתם.

In each *Partsuf*, there are interiority and exteriority, the exteriority is always of the aspect of *Mal'hut*, and the *Hechalot* are the ramifications of the Malhuts of the *Partsufim*. The *Hechalot* also have an aspect of interiority, which is the *Rua'h* in them.

Since the *Nukvah* [*Shekhina*] is the root of all the lower worlds and of the separated beings, she can not be complete without them. For the universal *Tikun,* it is necessary for all the separated beings to include in her. This is the principal function of the *Hechalot;* to allow the adhesion and attachment of all, in various and particular ways, until the *Hechal Kodesh Hakodashim.*

The *Neshamot* and the angels have their root in the *Hechalot,* each one depending on its respective level. The *Hechalot* are also the different levels of ascendance of the *Tefilot* before reaching the *'Olam Atsilut* (during the *Amidah*).

q) At the end[391] of *Atsilut,* there is a curtain; it is made from the lights of *Imah.*	יז. בסופו של אצילות - מסך, מאורה של אימא הוא נעשה .
[From this curtain] *Hashma'l* comes down and encircles *Z'uN* underneath its legs. The lights of *Atsilut* pass through it[392], and make *Beriah.* Thus, *Beriah* is of the [aspect] secret of *Imah.*	חשמ״ל יורד ומקיף מתחת רגליהם של זו״ן, ואורות של אצילות עוברים בו ועושים בריאה. נמצאה בריאה מסודה של אימא.
From it [*Beriah*] to *Yetsirah,* there are two curtains: A curtain from *Imah* to *Z'uN,* and a curtain from *Z'A* to *Nukvah.* Thus, *Yetsirah* is from the [aspect]	ממנה ליצירה מסך על מסך : מסך מאימא לזו״ן, ומסך מז״א לנוק׳. נמצאת יצירה מסודו של ז״א.

---

[391] At the bottom
[392] Curtain

secret of *Z'A*.

From it [*Yetsirah*] to *'Asiah*, one curtain on two [curtains]: One curtain from *Imah* to *Z'uN*, one curtain from *Z'A* to *Nukvah*, and one curtain from *Nukvah* to the world under her. Thus, *'Asiah* is of from the [aspect] secret of *Nukvah*.	ממנה לעשייה מסך על שנים : מסך מאי' לזו"ן, ומסך מז"א לנוקבא, מסך מנוק' לעולם שתחתיה . נמצאת עשייה מסודה של נוק ' .

At the bottom of *Atsilut*, a curtain is made from the striking of the lights. Through this curtain, the *Sephirot* come out from the higher world to the world under it. *Beriah* corresponds to *Imah*, *Yetsirah* to *Z'A,* and *'Asiah* to *Nukvah*.

r) The name of *Atsilut* is[393] *'AV*.	יח. שמו של אצילות - ע"ב.
SaG, MaH and *BaN* descended [394] to *Beriah, Yetsirah* and *'Asiah*. They returned and ascended: *MaH* ascended and clothed *SaG, BaN* ascended and clothed *MaH*.	ירדו ס"ג מ"ה ב"ן לבי"ע. חזרו ועלו. עלה מ"ה והלביש על ס"ג, עלה ב"ן והלביש על מ"ה.

---

[393] From the aspect of the name of *'AV* – miluy of 72
[394] When the *Kelim* broke

Thus, *BaN* is on top of all, this is the *Mahakey* [395] [מעקה], [a fence] for the endings of the lights not to be uncovered when they are below, so that the *Klipot*[396] will not attach to them. As it is said:

"You shall make a parapet for your roof, that you should not bring any blood upon your house, if any man falls from there" (Devarim, 22, 8)

נמצא ב״ן למעלה מכולן, זה מעקה,

שלא יהיה סיומם של אורות כשהם למטה,

ולא יהיו הקליפות אוחזות בהם, שנאמר (דברים כב, ח):
"ועשית מעקה לגגך ולא תשים דמים בביתך כי יפול הנופל ממנו".

The world of *Atsilut* is of the aspect of the name of *'AV,* *Beriah* is of the aspect of *SaG, Yetsirah* of the aspect of *MaH,* and *'Asiah* of the aspect of *BaN.*

When the *Kelim* broke, *SaG, MaH* and *BaN* descended to the lower worlds, *SaG* in *Beriah, MaH* in *Yetsirah,* and *BaN* in *'Asiah.* They came back up to be under the curtain of *Atsilut,* and *BaN* made the מעקה (parapet) on top of them, so that the *Klipot* will not attach to the higher lights.

s) These are the four worlds on which the Lord solely reigns, on all his work. The service of the creatures is in

יט. אלו ד׳ עולמות שבהם מולך אדון יחיד על מעשיו. עבודתם של תחתונים בכולם. ויחודו של א״ס ב״ה מתיחד

---

[395] Parapet or railing
[396] Husks (negative forces)

all of them [397]. The uniqueness [יקוק] of the *Ein Sof B'H*, is sovereign over all[398]. Like the master of the prophets said: "Hear Israel H' is our G-d H' is One" (Devarim, 10, 4)	בכולם. הוא שרבן של נביאים אומר (דברים י, ד): "שמע ישראל ה' אלהינו ה' אחד."

The goal of the divine service of the creatures, is to help prepare the *Partsufim Z'A* and *Nukvah* for the *Zivug,* and this by the elevation and adhesion of the worlds of *Beriah, Yetsirah* and *'Asiah* to the *Hechalot* of *Nukvah* of *Atsilut.*

---

[397] To make the *Tikun* of all the worlds
[398] The four worlds

Ninth chapter

The angels, the *Sitra A'hra*

Introduction

The Sephirot have their root from the Kedusha of the Ein Sof, B'H. The root of evil is in the absence, or great diminution of the Kedusha. This other entity, called Sitra A'hra – (the other side, or negative force), is the opposite world, with its four worlds, Sephirot, and destructive angels.

| a) From the *Sephirot,* there are three ramifications: the angels, the *Sitra A'hra,* and *Neshamot* (physical entities). For each mission, there is one angel. The *Sephirot* decree; the angels accomplish. As it is said: "Bless the Lord, O you his angels, you mighty ones, who do His word, listening to the voice of His word" (Tehilim, 103, 20) | א. תולדותיהם של ספירות ג' : מלאכים, סטרא אחרא (גשמים) [ונשמות]. לכל שליחות - מלאך. הספירות גוזרות והמלאך עושה, שנאמר (תהלים קג, כ) : "ברכו ה' מלאכיו גבורי כח עושי דברו לשמוע בקול דברו". |

As there are interior and exterior aspects for the *Sephirot,* there is a general interior aspect; which is the spiritual entity, and a general exterior aspect; which is the physical. The three superior worlds of *Atsilut, Beriah* and *Yetsirah,* are interior to the fourth world of *'Asiah.*

The *Neshamot* derive from the world of *Beriah,* the angels from the world of *Yetsirah,* and the physical from the world of *'Asiah.*

There is another entity, which is called the *Sitra A'hra* – (the other side, or the negative force). It is the opposite world, which also has its four worlds of *Atsilut, Beriah, Yetsirah* and *'Asiah.* Its destructive angels, depending on their importance, are from its own worlds of *Beriah, Yetsirah* or *'Asiah.*

b) The *Sitra A'hra,* how [is it built]? As it is said: "I form the light, and create darkness; I make peace, and create evil". (Isaiah, 45, 7) He forms the light; this is the right, He creates the obscurity; this is the left, He makes peace; these are the angels of peace, and creates evil; this is S'M[399].

ב. ס״א כיצד -
זהו שנאמר (ישעיה מה, ז):
"יוצר אור ובורא חושך עושה
שלום ובורא רע".
יוצר אור - זה הימין,
ובורא חושך - זהו בשמאל,
עושה שלום - אלו מלאכי שלום,
ובורא רע - זה סמ׳

The angels of peace make ten groups; they serve the ten *Sephirot* of the right. The angels of destruction make ten levels; they serve the ten *Sephirot* from the left side[400]. About them, he says: "G-d also made this one, facing the other" (Kohelet, 7, 14)

מלאכי שלום - עשר כתות,
משמשין לעשר ספירות של ימין.
מלאכי חבלה - עשר מדריגות,
משמשין לעשר ספירות מצד
שמאל.
עליהם הוא אומר (קהלת ז, יד):
"גם את זה לעומת זה עשה
האלהים".

The ten groups of positive angels are divided as follows: Three groups in *Beriah,* six groups in *Yetsirah,* and one group in *'Asiah.* The negative angels subdivide in the same order as well. The positive angels are also divided in the four camps of Michael, Gabriel, Ouriel, and Raphael.

---

[399] Initials of the main negative angel
[400] The lower side, (opposite side)

c) Four levels - four *Klipot* (husks); these are the worlds of *S'M*; they obstruct the lights of the *Sephirot*, and conceal him [401] . Because of the [bad] deeds of the lower beings, [402] they[403] come and do evil in the world.

[There are four *Klipot*]:

- נגה - (*Nogah*) - Glow

- ענן דול - (Anan Gadol) - A large cloud

- אש מתלקחת - (Eish Mitlakahat) - A dividing fire

- רוח סערה - (*Rua'h* Sehara) - A wind of storm.

As it is written in Ezekhiel: "And I looked, and behold, a stormy wind came from the north, a great cloud, a fire flaring up, and a glow was around it, and out of its midst; like the *Hashma'l*" (Ezekiel, 1, 4)

ג. ד' מדריגות - ד' קליפות,
עולמיו של סמ',
סותמים אורם של ספירות
ומסלקים אותו,
במעשה התחתונים באים,
ועושים רעה בעולם :

נוגה,

ענן גדול,

ואש מתלקחת,

ורוח סערה ;

שכן מפורשים ע"י יחזקאל (א, ד) :
"וארא והנה רוח סערה באה
מן־הצפון ענן גדול
ואש מתלקחת ונגה לו סבקב
ומתוכה כעקן החשמל מתוך האש"

---

[401] They conceal man from his root, and from the light
[402] Man
[403] The destructive angels

The *Sephirot* have their root in the *Kedusha* of the *Ein Sof*, *B'H*. The root of the *Sitra A'hra* is in the lack, or absence of the *Kedusha*. Its existence was willed by the Creator to give man free will. She[404] almost constantly tries to seduce him, and make him stumble.

When men are doing the will of their Creator, positive forces reach the higher realms and give strength to the *'Hasadim* to bestow goodness. However, when they are not doing His will, and sin, the negative forces get strength to attach to the exteriority of the *Sephirot*, to nourish from their lights, and to gain more power to act negatively.

d) Four *Klipot* - four worlds for each. In them [each world]; there are five *Partsufim* in ten *Sephirot*.	ד. ד׳ קליפות - ד׳ עולמות לכל אחת, שבם ה׳ פרצופים בעשר ספירות,
The *Tikunim* of the lower beings are in the four [superior] worlds [of *ABYA*], and the deterioration [they cause] reach the four [lower] worlds. If the lower beings merit, the Lord guides with mercy, and the "policeman" disregards. If they sin, the	שתיקוניהם של תחתונים בד׳ עולמות, ופגמיהם בד׳ עולמות. זכו התחתונים - האדון מנהג ברחמים, והשוטר עובר מפניו. חטאו - בעל הרחמים נסתלק, והשוטר עושה דין בחייבים. בסילוקו של אדון מעשהו של

---

[404] The *Sitra A'hra*

| Merciful departs, and the "policeman" acts with rigor on the guilty. It is only when the Lord departs, that the "policeman" acts. As it is said: "The anger of the Lord was kindled against them, and He departed, the cloud left the tent, and behold, Miriam had become leprous, white as snow." (Bamidbar, 12, 9, 10) | שוטר, הוא שנאמר (במדבר יב, ט-י) : "ויחר אף ה' בם וילך והענן סר מעל האהל והנה מרים מצורעת כשלג". |

The *Sitra A'hra* has four worlds that correspond to *ABYA*, it also has five *Partsufim, Sephirot, Hechalot* and angels, as in the positive world, but of a lower force.

The good deeds of man have an effect on the four higher worlds, his bad deeds; on the four lower worlds. It is only when man sins, that the negative side can grow in strength. The negative aspect grows inside him; this is his *Yetser Harah,* it cuts him off from the higher worlds, and uproots him from the *Kedusha.*

| e) The roots of the *Klipot*[405] proceed from the order of the rigors[406]. By them[407]; | ה. סדרי הדינים - אלה שרשים של קליפות, מהם מכניעים אותה, ומהם - |

---

[405] This root is from the side of the *Kedusha*

[406] The rears of the *Sephirot*

[407] The rears of the *Sephirot*

she is subdued, and by them, she is amplified depending on the deeds of the lower beings. As it is written: "You shall therefore keep My statutes, and My judgments; which if a man does, he shall live in them" (Vayikra, 18, 5)	מגביהים אותה, לפי מעשיהם של תחתונים. הוא שהכתוב אומר (ויקרא יח, ה) : "ושמרתם את חוקותי ואת משפטי אשר יעשה אותם האדם וחי בהם".

From the names of *Elokim,* which are the lights of the aspects of the rears; the *Klipot* get their strength. However, the root of evil has its origin from the positive side; it is of course certain, that no other force can exist without the permission of G-d *B'H.*

Evil will disappear from this world and change to goodness, when the *Tikunim* will be completed. Consequently, these rigors will be appeased, and the *Sitra A'hra* will not be able to attach to the higher lights anymore.

By giving man a role in the general *Tikun,* it is now up to him to restore, and make the necessary reparations to the world. However, if man does not act accordingly, the *Tikun* will still be realized, but in the time set by the Creator.

Tenth chapter

The souls

Introduction

The soul has five names: Nefesh, Rua'h, Neshama, 'Hayah and Ye'hidah. The soul is the spiritual entity inside the body, the latter being only his outer garment. The Tikun of the soul is realized by the Gilgul (reincarnation), and by the Ibur (attachment).By accomplishing what he did not accomplish of the 613 Mitsvot, man makes the necessary Tikun of his soul, which can now elevate to the higher realms, and rejoin its source.

a) The service to the Lord is done by the souls. It has five names: *Nefesh, Rua'h, Neshama, 'Hayah* and *Ye'hidah,* [their roots are] from the five *Partsufim.* *'Hayah* and *Ye'hidah* are from *Atsilut, Neshama* from *Beriah, Rua'h* from *Yetsirah,* and *Nefesh* from *'Asiah.*

א. עבודתו של מקום - לנשמות.
ה' שמות הם : נר"נ ח"י, מה'
פרצופים.
חיה יחידה מאצילות,
נשמה מבריאה,
רוח מיצירה,
נפש מעשייה.

Therefore, the force of man is from *Mal'hut* of *'Asiah,* until *Keter* of *Atsilut.* As it is said: "Let Us make man in Our image, after Our likeness; and let them have dominion over the creatures of the sea ..." (Bereshit, 1, 26)

נמצא כחו של אדם
ממלכותו של עשייה עד כתרו של
אצילות.
זהו שנאמר (בראשית א, כו) :
"נעשה אדם בצלמנו כדמותנו
וירדו בדגת הים".

The soul has five names: *Nefesh, Rua'h, Neshama, 'Hayah* and *Ye'hidah,* which correspond to its five levels. The soul is the spiritual entity inside the body. Since it is men that provoke the union of the four worlds, it is necessary for their souls to have their origin from them.

All the souls of the level of *Nefesh* are from *'Asiah,* the ones of the level of *Rua'h* are from *Yetsirah,* of the level of *Neshama* from *Beriah,* and of the level of *'Hayah* and *Ye'hidah* from

Atsilut. Since there are in each world *Partsufim* and *Sephirot*, each soul has its origin corresponding to one of these various levels. Therefore, a soul could be from the level of *Mal'hut* of *'Asiah, Abah* of *'Asiah, Z'A* of *Yetsirah,* or *Imah* of *Beriah* etc.

The higher levels of the soul cannot be acquired at once. Most men only have the level of *Nefesh,* and if they merit, they will acquire the next levels - but one by one.

To reach the next higher level of his soul, man must do the *Tikun* of the preceding level. If he needs to acquire the level of *Imah* of *'Asiah,* he must first do the *Tikun* of *Mal'hut* of *'Asiah* and *Z'A* of *'Asiah,* and so on. To acquire his level of *Neshama,* he must do the *Tikun* of all the levels of the *Sephirot* and *Partsufim*[408] of his *Nefesh* and *Rua'h*.

b) The *Tikun* of the soul is realized by the *Gilgul* [reincarnation], and the *Ibur* [attachment].	‫ב. תיקוניה של נשמה - גלגול‬ ‫ועיבור.‬
How? The service of the soul is the accomplishment of the 613 *Mitsvot,* if it accomplishes them; it ascends to rest, if not; it comes back and reincarnates. It does not reincarnate completely, only its parts that need the	‫כיצד ?‬ ‫עבודתה של נשמה תרי״ג מצוות,‬ ‫השלימתם - עולה למנוחה,‬ ‫ואם לאו - חוזרת ומתגלגלת.‬ ‫לא כולה מתגלגלת,‬ ‫אלא חלקיה הצריכים תיקון .‬

---

[408] Of the levels of the worlds of *'Asiah* and *Yetsirah*

Tikun do.

If man does not do the *Tikun* of the level of his soul for which he came; he comes back and reincarnates. It is by accomplishing what he did not accomplish of the 613 *Mitsvot*, that he makes the needed *Tikun*. Therefore, it is not all the soul that comes back, but only the parts that need to be repaired [by doing the missing *Mitsva*], come again. There are 613 parts to the soul, similarly, there are 613 *Mitsvot*, and 613 veins and bones to man, this number is not arbitrary, as there are important interrelations and interactions between them[409].

c) What is a *Gilgul*, and what is an *Ibur*: The *Gilgul* is [the reincarnation of a soul] from the time of birth until death, the *Ibur* [is an attachment of another soul to his, which] could come and leave anytime.	ג. איזהו גלגול ואיזהו עיבור ? גלגול - משעת לידה ועד מיתה ; עיבור - ביאתו בכל שעה, ויציאתו בכל שעה.
For the *Mitsvot* that it was obligated to accomplish, it accomplishes them by the *Gilgul*, for the ones it did not have to accomplish,[410] it accomplishes them by the *Ibur*, which departs	מצוות שנתחייבה בהם - משלימתם בגלגול, ושלא נתחייבה בהם - בעיבור משלימתם, והולכת לה.

---

[409] *Mitsvot* – soul - body

[410] *Mitsvot* that were not possible for him to accomplish as: Circumcision for a son he did not have etc.

afterwards.

The *Tsadikim* reincarnate up to a thousand generations, the sinners; up to four. As it is said "But for the fourth I will not turn away." (Amos, 1, 3)	צדיקים מתגלגלים לאלפים, רשעים עד רבעים, שנא' (עמוס א, ג) : "ועל ארבעה לא אשיבנו".

The soul given to man at his birth stays with him all his life. To help him accomplish the missing *Mitsva*, another soul could attach to his soul [*Ibur*], until he accomplishes it, and then departs. The missing *Mitsva* could be one he chose not to do, or one he could not do in his previous life.

If one undertakes the *Tikun* of his soul in three reincarnations, he will come back again as needed, to complete his *Tikun*. However, if he maintains his wrong behavior, he will not come back after the third reincarnation.

d) *Nefesh* comes first, after it comes *Rua'h*, after it *Neshama*, and after them come *'Hayah* and *Ye'hidah*. There are garments [envelopes] for each soul. *Nefesh*, *Rua'h* and *Neshama* reincarnate independently.	ד. נפש בא בתחלה, ואחריו רוח, ואחריו נשמה, וח"יי אחריהן. לכל נשמה לבושים. מתגלגלת נפש לבדה ורוח לבדו ונשמה לבדה.
Souls could mount on garments [envelopes] not of their sort. Not all the souls	ומרכיבים נשמות בלבושים שלא במינם. לא כל הנשמות שוות :

are equal, the new are not like the old, and the reincarnated once is not like the reincarnated twice. On all [these souls], it is written:
"And it is turned around by His guidance, so that they may do whatever He commands them ..." (Job, 37, 12)

שלא כחדשות הישנות,
ולא כמגולגלות אחת המגולגלות שתים.
ועל כולם הוא אומר (איוב לז, יב):

"והוא מסבות מתהפך בתחבולותיו לפעלם".

"But devises means, that none of us be banished".
(Samuel 2, 14, 14)

ואומר (שמואל ב יד, יד):
"וחשב מחשבות לבלתי ידח ממנו נדח".

"Every one who is called by My Name; for I have created him for My glory, I have formed him; yes, I have made him".
(Isaiah, 43, 7)

ואומר (ישעיה מג, ז):
"כל הנקרא בשמי ולכבודי בראתיו יצרתיו אף עשיתיו".

"G-od will reign forever".
(Shemot, 16, 18)

ואומר (שמות טו, יח):
"ה' ימלוך לעולם ועד".

"And your people shall all be Tsadikim; and possess this land forever, a branch of My planting, a work of My hands; for My proudness"

ואומר (ישעיה ס, כא):
"ועמך כולם צדיקים לעולם ירשו ארץ
נצר מטעי מעשי ידי להתפאר".

The garment [*Levush*] or envelop, is what is necessary for the soul to attach to the body of man. When another soul attaches to him, it could use the same *Levush* to remain in him. New souls are the ones that have not come yet, old souls have come before.

In the beginning, all the souls were inside *Adam Harishon*, when he sinned; some fell down to the *Klipot*, and some remained in him. The main difference is that only the new souls have the possibility to make the *Tikun* of all the levels at once. The older souls could be reincarnated in separate parts, and in many reincarnations, to acquire all the levels of *Rua'h* and *Neshama*.

Finally, all these complex possibilities have only one purpose: To allow man to merit by his own efforts, to get closer to his Creator, and live the *Dvekut* – the adhesion with G-d. In this way, man will attain perfection and be directly involved in the ultimate goal of the creation, which is the revelation of G-d's Sovereignty – *Giluy Yehudo*.

Baroukh Hachem, Leholam, Amen Veamen.

Complete text

First chapter

a) Until the world was created, He and His Name were One.

He willed [to create], and contracted His light to create all beings, by giving them a space. There is no existence that does not have its space.

The space [from where the light contracted] being circular, the *Ein Sof* [411] encircles it from all sides.

A ray [*Kav*] emerged from Him, entered on one side, and made all the levels[412].

They [The *Sephirot*] are ten levels, with incommensurable qualities. Ten encircling, and in their middle, ten linear, which have the qualities of the *Ein Sof:* kindness, rigor and

פרק ראשון

א. עד שלא נברא העולם היה הוא ושמו אחד.
רצה וצמצם אורו לברוא כל הבריות, נתן להם מקום.
אין לך דבר שאין לו מקום.

נמצא המקום שווה לכולם.
והאין סוף ב"ה מקיפו לכל צד.
וקו יוצא ממנו לצד אחד, בוקע ונכנס, ועושה כל המדרגות.

עשר מדרגות הן, מדתן שאין להם סוף.
עשרה עגולים, ויושרם באמצעם,
שבהם מידותיו של מקום –
חסד, דין, רחמים.

---

[411] The infinite, literally, "without end"
[412] *Sephirot*

mercy.

He directs His creatures
with justice, rewarding and
punishing, returning all evil
to goodness, and bringing
all His creatures to His will.
As it is written:
"I am first and I am last, and
beside Me there is no G-d."
(Isaiah, 44, 6).

מנהג כל בריותיו במשפט,
משכיר ומעניש,
ומחזיר כל רעה לטובה,
ומביא בריותיו לרצונו.
וכן הוא אומר (ישעיה מד, י) :
"אני ראשון ואני אחרון
ומבלעדי אין אלהים". (כז-כח)

All that G-d created in His
world, He created only for
His glory, as it is said:
"All that is called by My
Name and glory, I created,
formed and even made."
(Isaiah, 43, 7).
And He said: "G-d will
reign for ever." (Shemot, 15,
18)

כל מה שברא הקב״ה בעולמו
לא בראו אלא לכבודו,
שנאמר (ישעיה מג, ז) :
"כל הנקרא בשמי ולכבודי
בראתיו יצרתיו אף עשיתיו".
ואומר (שמות טו, יח) :
"ה' ימלוך לעולם ועד" .

b) Ten *Sephirot,* internal and
external; their shape, as of a
man[413], the first of them;
Adam Kadmon (Primordial
Man). From the lights that
were invested inside of him,

ב. עשר ספירות פנימיות
וחיצוניות דמיונן כמראה אדם.
הראשון שבכולם - אדם קדמון.
וממה שנגבל בפנים
יוצאים ארבע חושים חלק
ממנו : רשר״יד. (כט)

---

[413] The shape of the *Sephirot*ic tree resembles the shape of man

came out [ramifications] his four senses: Sight, hearing, smell and speech.

c) From the four letters of הוי"ה ב"ה, there are Four Miluim:
- ע"ב, ס"ג, מ"ה, ב"ן ('AV, SaG, MaH, BaN)
- *Ta'amim* [cantillation notes]
- *Nekudot* [vowels]
- *Tagin* [crowns]
- *Autiot* [letters]
They include one, in the other[414].

ע"ב ('AV) is in the head, its ramifications are mysterious; they come out from the hair on the head.

ס"ג (SaG) came out from the ears and downward. Its cantillation notes subdivide in three levels: Higher, middle and lower. The

ג. תיות הוי"ה ב"ה ד' או
ד' מלואים: עסמ"ב טנת"א
ע"ב ,ס"ג ,מ"ה, ב"ן
טנת"א
טעמים.
נקודות
תגין
אותיות
נכללים אלו מאלו

ע"ב בגולגולת, ענפיו נעלמים,
מן השערות של הראש הם
יוצאים.

יצא ס"ג מן האזנים ולמטה.
טעמים שלו ג' מינים :
עליונים, תחתונים, אמצעים.

---

[414] The *Ta'amim* correspond to the name of *'AV*, the *Nekoudot* to the name of *SaG*, *the Tagin* to *MaH,* and the *Autiot* to *BaN*. The *Ta'amim* also have an aspect of *SaG* (*SaG* of *'AV*) and so on
[415] The *Sephirot*

higher [are] from the ears, the middle from the nose, and the lower from the mouth.

עליונים באזנים,
אמצעים בחוטם,
תחתונים בפה

The higher came out from the ears, ten [*Sephirot*] from the right, and ten [*Sephirot*] from the left, these internal, and these encircling. They all include in one ה, which is shaped as ו ד. How far do they descend? Until the end of the beard on the chin.

יצאו עליונים מן האזנים,
עשרה מהימין ועשרה מהשמאל,
אלו פנימים ואלו מקיפים לגביהם,
כלולים בה׳ אחת שצורתה ד״ו.
עד היכן הם יורדין ?
עד כנגד שבולת הזקן.

The middle, came out from the nose, ten [*Sephirot*] from the right, and ten from the left, these internal, and these encircling. They approached[415] each other, and then the ו of the ה was revealed, with six *Alephs*, [א א א א א א] coming out and downward, reaching to the chest.

יצאו אמצעים מן החוטם,
עשרה מימין, ועשרה משמאל,
אלו פנימים, ואלו מקיפים
לגביהם.
והרי נתקרבו זה לגבי זה,
ונתגלתה ו׳ של ה׳ בששה אלפין
[א א א א א א].
יוצאים ויורדין עד החזה.

The lower [*Ta'amim*] came out from the mouth, ten internal [*Sephirot*], and ten encircling [*Sephirot*], in this way was revealed the ד of

יצאו התחתונים מן הפה,
י׳ פנימים וי׳ מקיפים,
ונתגלתה הד׳ שבה׳ בד׳ אלפין,
שנים יו׳י, ושנים יוד.

the ה, with four Aleph, [א א א א] two יי, and two יוד.

From the two ears and the two nostrils; two vapors from the right side of the mouth, and two utterances from the left side, they are rooted in the two jaws, upper and lower. They come out, and descend until the navel.

מב' אזנים ומב' נחירים – ב' הבלים בימינו של הפה ושני דיבורים בשמאלו, נשרשים בב' לחיים - עליון ותחתון. יוצאין ויורדין עד הטבור.

d) Mal'hut came out[416] first, followed by Z'A, and than the others [Sephirot until Keter]. The force [the consistence] of the Keli was absorbed in them[417].

ד. יצאו ראשונה, מלכות בתחלה, וז"א אחריה, וכן כולם. וכח הכלי בלוע בהם.

The most tenuous [418] returned and entered [419], Keter first, followed by the others. The rest [which did not return] thickened. A Keli was made from the

הדק שבהם חזר ונכנס, כתר בתחלה וכולם אחריו. נתעבה הנשאר, ונעשה כלי מניצוצות שנפלו בו מהכאת אור חזרתו של עליון ורשימו של תחתון.

---

[416] From the mouth of *Adam Kadmon*
[417] The lights of the mouth of *Adam Kadmon*
[418] Of the lights
[419] In the mouth of *Adam Kadmon*

sparks that fell from the collision of the returning higher light, with the trace[420] of the lower [light].

At first, they were all [of the aspect of] Nefashot. They gained from each other by coming out, and by returning; each one as it deserved, until the second encircling[421]. *Keter* stayed in the mouth of A`K, the nine remaining [*Sephirot*] came out, until *Mal'hut* was left as a *Keli* without light.

בראשונה היו כלם נפשות.
הרויחו זה מזה ביציאתם וכן בחזרתם,
כל אחד כראוי לו, עד מקיף שני.
נשאר הכתר בפה דא״ק,
ושאר התשעה יצאו,
עד שנמצאת מלכות כלי בלי אור.

All the *Kelim* made one [unique] *Keli*, but with ten gradations. This is the [world of] Ha'Akudim.[422]

כל הכלים כלי אחד,
אלא שעשר שנתות יש לו,
זה עקודים.

---

[420] Each light when going up, leaves a trace (imprint)
[421] For *Mal'hut* only
[422] Attached

Second chapter

a) The vowels of *SaG* being ready to come out, *SaG* assembled his own *MaH* and *BaN* [423] , and [the general] *MaH* and *BaN* with them, from the navel and up. It spread there a curtain [a limit], starting in the front at the level of his chest, and extending down to his rear until the level of his navel.

From *BaN*; *Sephirot* ascended and came out trough the eyes [of *Adam* Kadmon]: Ten [*Sephirot*] from the right, and ten from the left. They [the *Kelim*] came out from the navel, and downward. They [the *Sephirot*] took from the higher lights, *KHB* [424] [received from the lights] of the ears, nose and mouth that were on the beard of the chin, and the rest [the

---

[423] *MaH* of *SaG* and *BaN* of *SaG*
[424] *Keter*, *'Hokhma* and *Binah*

פרק שני

א. עמדו נקודותיו לצאת,
אסף ס״ג המ״ה וב״ן שלו,
ומ״ה וב״ן עמהם,
מן הטבור ולמעלה;
ופרש שם מסך,
מתחיל מלפניו בחזה,
ומשפע ויורד מאחריו,
עד כנגד הטבור.

ומן הב״ן עלו ויצאו מן העינים
עשר ספירות מן הימין, ועשר מן
השמאל.
יצאו וירדו מן הטבור ולמטה,
ולקחו אור ממה שלמעלה:
כח״ב מאח״פ בשבלתה של זקן,
והשאר מן הפה משם ולמטה.

seven lower *Sephirot* received from the lights] of the mouth and lower [the beard on the chin].

From the inside [of *Adam Kadmon*], BaN descended, cleaved out at their level [of the lights of the eyes that went down] and shone outwards through his skin [of *Adam Kadmon*]. From the navel and the *Yesod* [of *Adam Kadmon*] the light divided to *Keter*, *'Hokhma* and *Binah*, the remaining [the seven lower *Sephirot*, received from the lights] of the toes.

ומבפנים ירד ובקע ב"ן כנגדם,
והאיר דרך עורו לחוץ.
מן הטבור ומן היסוד
נחלקת אור לכתר ולחו"ב,
והשאר מאצבעותיהם של רגלים.

The three first ones were repaired, facing each other, the rest [seven lower *Sephirot*] were one under the other.

נמצא:
ג' ראשונות מתוקנים זה כנגד זה,
והשאר זה תחת זה .

b) Ten *Kelim* came out first, and afterwards, their lights. The lights went down to *Keter*, *'Hokhma* and *Binah* and were accepted; but by the seven lower ones, they

ב. יצאו עשרה כלים בראשונה,
ואורותיהם אח"כ.
ירדו האורות לכח"ב וקבלום;
לז"ת ולא קבלום.
ירדו כליהם למטה,
ואורותיהם עלו למקומם.

were not accepted. Their *Kelim* went down [to *Beriah*, *Yetsirah* and *'Asiah*], and their lights ascended to their place [in *Atsilut*].

On them, it is written:

"And these are the kings who reigned in the land of Edom, before reigned a king over the children of Israel" (Bereshit, 36, 31).

c) Ten *Sephirot* [of *Nekudim*] to be divided into six *Partsufim* [in *Atsilut*], and from them, four worlds: *Atsilut*, *Beriah*, *Yetsirah* and *'Asiah*. From their extremity [of these levels][425] comes out evil, as it is said:

"I form the light, and create darkness; I make peace, and create evil". (Isaiah, 45, 7)

The sparks have no attachments between them.

ועליהם הוא אומר (בראשית לו,
לא) :
"ואלה המלכים אשר מלכו בארץ
אדום
לפני מלך מלך לבני
ישראל".

ג. עשר ספירות עומדות ליחלק
בששה פרצופים,
ומהם נעשו ד' עולמות – אבי״ע
ומסופם יוצא הרע,
שנאמר (ישעיה מה, ז) :
"יוצר אור ובורא חושך עושה
שלום ובורא רע".

זיקין ניצוצים אין ביניהם חיבור,
שנאמר (משלי טז, כח) :

---

[425] *Mal'hut* of *'Asiah*

As it is said:
"A whisperer separates close friends" (Michleh, 16, 28)

"ונרגן מפריד אלוף".

And for the wicked he said:
"All the evil doers shall be scattered:" (Tehilim, 92, 10)

וברשעים הוא אומר (תהלים צב, י):
"יתפרדו כל פועלי און".

But for the saintly what does he say:
"And G-d will be king on all the land, on this day G-d will be One and His Name One" (Zachariah, 14, 9)

אבל בקדושה מה הוא אומר (זכריה יד, ט):
"והיה ה' למלך על כל הארץ ביום ההוא יהיה ה' אחד ושמו אחד" –

Because the *Tikun* of everything; is by the unity [*Yihud*].

שתיקון הכל ביחוד

d) In the beginning, all the parts [of the *Kelim*] were equal. The lights came out but were not accepted [by Z'aT[426]]; they [the *Kelim*] broke and fell. The finest [of the lights] were

ד. בתחלה היו כל החלקים שוים. באו האורות ולא קיבלום, נשברו ונפלו. נגנז המעולה שבהם, ומן הנשאר ירד הטוב שבו לבריאה, ושלאחריו ליצירה,

---

[426] *Zain Tahtonim* – The seven lower *Sephirot*
[427] From the three worlds of *Beriah*, *Yetsirah* and *'Asiah*, were made the four worlds of *Atsilut*, *Beriah*, *Yetsirah* and *'Asiah*
[428] *Mal'hut* of the second *'Asiah*

concealed, and the best of those remaining [of the *Kelim*] descended to *Beriah*, the rest to *Yetsirah* and *'Asiah*.

ושלאחריו לעשיה.

When they [the *Kelim*] came back and were repaired; four were made of three[427]. The second *'Asiah* is lower than the first, and from its extremity[428], evil comes out. As the prophet said:

"Behold, I will make you small among the nations; you shall be greatly despised" (Ovadia, 1, 2)

כשחזרו ונתקנו, נעשה מג׳ ד׳.
נמצאת עשיה השניה תחתונה
מהראשונה.
ומסופה הרע יוצא,
הוא שהנביא אמר (עובדיה א, ב) :
"קטן נתתיך בגוים בזוי אתה מאד"

e) Which[429] ones went down? The seven lower ones[430] and the rears of *'Hokhma* and *Binah*. The seven lower went down to *Beriah*, the rears of *'Hokhma* and *Binah* went down to the place of *Z'uN*

ה. מי הם היורדים ?
ז״ת, ואחוריהם של חו״ב;
אלא שז״ת ירדו לבריאה,
ואחוריהם של חו״ב למקום זו״ן
שבאצילות :
אחורי חכמה מלפניהם
ואחורי בינה מאחוריהם.
ז״ת נשברו;

---

[429] *Kelim*

[430] *Sephirot*

[431] Being still in the world of *Nekudim*, the concept of *Partsuf* does not exist yet, we are then talking about the world of *Tikun*

in *Atsilut*, the rears of
'Hokhma in front, and those
of *Binah* in the back [back
to back]. The seven lower
ones broke, but the rears of
'Hokhma and *Binah* did not;
they only fell. The rears of
NHY of *Keter* were also
damaged with them.

In every *Partsuf*, the seven
lower [*Sephirot*] broke, the
rears of *'Hokhma* and *Binah*
fell, and the rears of *NHY* of
Keter were damaged.
Of which *Partsufim*? The
ones that will come after[431].

f) How did they [*Z'aT*] fall?

The first one [to fall] was
Da'at, it received seven
lights [from *Z'aT* of
Nekudim] but could not
hold them; it broke and fell.
Its *Keli* [fell] to *Da'at* of
Beriah, and its light to

ואחורי חו"ב לא נשברו אלא נפלו ;
ואחורי נה"י של כתר נפגמו עמהם.

נמצאו :
ז"ת שבכל פרצוף שבורים,
ואחורי חו"ב נפולים,
ושל נה"יי של כתר פגומים.
באיזה פרצופין דברו ?
באותן שלאחר כך

ו. כיצד נפלו ?

ראשון שבכולם **דעת,**
קבל ז' אורות, ולא עמד בהם,
נשבר ונפל,
כליו בדעת דבריאה,
ואור שלו במלכות דאצילות.

---

[432] Being of the same column, (central)
[433] The light of *Daat*
[434] Of *Daat*
[435] Being of the same column, (left)

Mal'hut of Atsilut.

Afterwards, 'Hesed received six lights; it broke and fell. Its Keli fell to Binah of Beriah, and its light to Yesod of Atsilut.

קבל **חסד** אחריו ששה אורות נשבר ונפל,
כליו בבינה דבראה,
ואור שלו ביסוד דאצילות.

Gevurah received in the same way; it broke and fell. Its Keli fell to 'Hokhma of Beriah, and its light to Netsah and Hod of Atsilut.

קבלה **גבורה** על דרך זה, נשברה ונפלה,
כליה בחכמה דבריאה,
ואורה בנ"ה דאצילות.

Tiferet received in the same way; it broke and fell. Its Keli fell to Keter of Beriah, and its light remained in place. The Keli of Keter extended [432] and received it[433], the light of Da'at went up between them, and its Keli[434] fell a second time, [but now] to Mal'hut of Beriah.

קבל **תפארת** על דרך זה, נשבר ונפל,
כליו בכתר דבריאה,
ואור שלו עמד במקומו.
נתפשט כלי הכתר וקיבלו.
ואור הדעת עלה ביניהם,
ונפל כלי שלו שניה עד המלכות דבריאה.

---

[436] The light of Gevurah
[437] Of Gevurah
[438] Being of the same column, (right)
[439] The light of 'Hesed
[440] Of 'Hesed

The lights went out to [the *Kelim* of] *Netsah* and *Hod*, there, they found the light of *Gevurah* that had fallen, [the *Keli* of] *Binah* extended [435] and received it [436], and its *Keli* [437] fell a second time, [but now] to *Yesod* of *Beriah*. *Netsah* and *Hod* received and broke; their *Kelim* [fell] to *Netsah* and *Hod* of *Beriah*, their lights went up to the *Keli* of *Binah*.

The lights went out to [the *Keli* of] *Yesod*, there, they found the light of *'Hesed*. *'Hokhma* extended [438] and received it [439], and its *Keli* [440] fell a second time [but now] to *Tiferet* of *Beriah*.

Yesod received, broke and fell; its *Keli* [fell] to *Gevurah* of *Beriah,* and its light went up to *Keter*.

Mal'hut received, broke and fell; its *Keli* [fell] to *'Hesed* of *Beriah,* and its light went up to *Keter*.

יצאו האורות לנ״ה.
מצאו שם אור הגבורה שנפלה.
נתפשטה הבינה וקבלתו,
וירד כליה שניה עד היסוד
דבריאה.
קבלו **נ״ה**, ונשברו,
ונפל כלים בנ״ה דבריאה,
ואורם עלה לכליה של בינה.

יצאו האורות ליסוד,
ומצאו שם אורו של חסד.
נתפשטה החכמה וקבלתו,
נפל כליו שניה עד התפארת.

קבל **היסוד**, נשבר ונפל,
כליו לגבורה דבריאה,
ואור שלו עלה לכתר.

קיבלה **המלכות**, נשברה ונפלה,
כליה לחסד דבריאה,
ואור שלה עלה לכתר.

This is the order of the breaking of the seven lower [*Sephirot*]. It is from them that the worlds of *Beriah*, *Yetsirah* and *'Asiah* were prepared, and constructed.

זה סדר שבירתם של ז"ת,
שבהם הוכנו ונעשו בי"ע.

g) The descent of the rears of *'Hokhma* and *Binah* was consequent to the breaking of the [seven] lower ones:

ז. ירידת אחוריים של חו"ב
לפי שבירתם של תחתונות.

'Hokhma and *Binah*[441] were face to face. [When] *Da'at* broke, the *'Hasadim* and *Gevurot* of *'Hokhma* and *Binah* fell into their body[442], they turned [443] [back to back]; so as not to look at each other.

חו"ב - פנים בפנים.
נשבר **דעת**,
ונפלו חו"ג שבחו"ב בגוף,
חזרו שלא להסתכל זה בזה.

'Hesed broke; the rears [*NHY*] of *Abah* descended to *Yesod* [of *Abah*]; his rears[444] turned from facing *Imah*.

נשבר **חסד**,
ירדו אחוריו של אבא עד היסוד,
והפך אחוריו לפני אימא.

---

[441] In the beginning
[442] From their heads, their *'Hasadim* and *Gevurot* fell into their bodies
[443] The heads of *Abah* and *Imah*
[444] Of his body, his head had turned already

Gevurah broke; the rears of *Imah* descended to *Yesod* [of *Imah*], they both turned[445] back to back.

נשברה **גבורה,**

ירדו אחוריה של אימא עד היסוד,

חזרו שניהם אחור באחור.

The third of *Tiferet* broke; the rears of the *Yesod*s of *Abah* and *Imah* descended.

נשבר **שלישו של תפארת,**

ירדו אחורי יסודיהם של או״א.

Tiferet broke completely; the 'Hasadim and *Gevurot* of *Israel Saba* and *Tevunah* descended in their bodies, they turned[446] so as not to look at each other.

גמר ת״ת להשבר,

ירדו חו״ג שביסו״ת בגופם,

חזרו שלא להסתכל זה בזה.

Netsah and *Hod* broke; the rears of *ISOT* descended until *Yesod*.

נשברו **נ״ה,**

ירדו אחוריהם של יסו״ת עד

היסוד.

Yesod broke; the rears of their *Yesod*s[447] fell.

נשבר **היסוד,**

נפלו אחורי יסודיהם.

Mal'hut broke; the rear of their crowns [448] [surrounding their *Yesod*s] fell, and the damage to [the rears of] *NHY* of *Keter* was

נשברה **מלכות,**

ירדו אחורי עטרותיהם.

ונשלם פגמם של נה״י דכתר,

שבהן נכנסין חו״ג בחו״ב.

---

[445] *Abah* and *Imah* are now back to back
[446] *ISOT*
[447] Of *ISOT*
[448] Of *ISOT*
[449] *NHY* of *Keter*

completed. It is by them[449]
that the *'Hasadim* and
Gevurot enter *'Hokhma* and
Binah.

h) The 288 sparks are lights
from the four *'AV*: *'AV* of
'AV, *'AV* of *SaG*, *'AV* of
MaH and *'AV* of *BaN*,
which went down with the
broken *Kelim* to sustain
them.

ח. ורפ״ח ניצוצין של אור
מארבעה ע״ב דעסמ״ב
ירדו עם הנשברים לקיימם.

What descended did so as a
result of the descent of the
Malkin[450] (kings), and what
returned and rose again did
so because of their return.

כל היורד - מירידתם של מלכים
הוא יורד,
וכל החוזר ועולה - מחזרתם הוא
חוזר.

At the end of things what
does he say: "And the
light of the moon will be as
the light of the sun... When
G-d will dress the wounds
of His people and heal its
bruise. "(Isaiah. 30 .26)

ובסופן של דברים מה הוא אומר
(ישעיה ל, כו):
"והיה אור הלבנה כאור החמה"
ואומר (שם):
"ביום חבוש ה' את שבר עמו
ומחץ מכתו ירפא"

A recovery which is not
followed by a blow: And he

רפואה שאין אחריה מכה;

---

[450] The seven kings of Edom that died, correspond to the *Z'aT* that broke

said:

"I will erase the sin of this land in one day." (Zachariah 3. 9). And he said:

"And G-d will be king on all the land, on this day G-d will be One and His Name One." (Zachariah 14. 9.)

ואומר (זכריה ג, ט) :

"ומשתי את עון הארץ ההיא ביום אחד";

ואומר (שם יד, ט) :
"והיה ה' למלך על כל הארץ ביום ההוא יהיה ה' אחד ושמו אחד". (מד)

Third chapter

a) *MaH*[451] came out through the forehead [of *Adam Kadmon*], it selected and made from all the broken *Kelim*[452] five *Partsufim* [*Arikh Anpin, Abah, Imah, Zeir Anpin* and *Nukvah*], and *'Atik* above them, and from the rears of *Abah* and *Imah*[453] [it made] *Ya'acov* and *Leah*.

From *Keter* of *MaH,* and from half of *Keter*[454] of *BaN,* and from what was needed from the rest[455]; *'Atik*[456] was realized.

From *'Hokhma* of *MaH,* and from half of *Keter*[457] of

פרק שלישי

א. יצא מ״ה מן המצח,
בירר לו ועשה מכל שבריהם של
כלים
חמשה פרצופים,
ועתיק שעל גביהם,
ומאחוריהם של או״א - יעקב
ולאה.

כתר דמ״ה וחצי כתר דב״ן,
ומן השאר הראוי לו לעתיק.

חכמה דמ״ה וחצי כתרו של ב״ן,
ומהשאר הראוי לו זה א״א.

---

[451] The ten *Sephirot* of *MaH*

[452] *Z'aT* of *BaN*

[453] Their *NHY* that fell, but still in *Atsilut*

[454] Five superior *Sephirot* of *Keter*

[455] Of the *Sephirot*

[456] *Atik* is the *Mal'hut* of *Adam Kadmon,* that enters *Atsilut* to attach it to him

[457] Five lower *Sephirot* of *Keter*

[458] By the union of the *Sephirot* of the masculine aspect – *MaH,* and the feminine aspect – *BaN*

BaN, and from what was needed from the rest, *Arikh Anpin* was realized.

From *Binah* of *MaH,* and from *'Hokhma* and *Binah* of *BaN,* and from what was needed from the rest, *Abah* and *Imah* were realized.

בינה דמ״ה וחו״ב של ב״ן,
ומהשאר הראוי להם - או״א.

From the seven lower *Sephirot* of *MaH,* and from the seven *Sephirot* of *BaN, Zeir Anpin* was realized.

וי״ק דמ״ה ווי״ק של ב״ן - ז״א.

From *Mal'hut* of *MaH,* and from *Mal'hut* of *BaN, Nukvah* was realized.

מלכותו של מ״ה ומלכותו של ב״ן -
נוק׳.

Their *Tikun* [rectification - arrangement] is achieved by the masculine and feminine[458] principles. They are repaired by *D'uN*[459] ; during the *Zivug,*[460] the gestation, the birth, and the growth.

תיקונם בזכר ונקבה.
ומדו״ן הם נתקנים :
בזיווג, עיבור, לידה, וגדלות.

---

[459] *Duchrin* and *Nukvin* - Aramaic for masculine and feminine. The *Partsuf* is repaired by the union of the masculine and feminine aspects of the *Partsuf* superior to him
[460] Union

b) The *Zivug*[461], in what manner [is it done]? [First] The *Nukvah* [of the upper *Partsuf*] brings up *Mayim Nukvin* [462] [feminine desire], which make the selection of the *Kelim*, and then in return; the lights [463] of *MaH* come down.

ב. בזיווג כיצד ?
מעלה נוק׳ מ״ן - בירוריהם של כלים,
ויורדים כנגדם אורותיו של מ״ה.

They stand [464] in *Nukvah* [465], and are repaired in her interior; this corresponds to the gestation ('Ibur).

עומדים בנוק׳ ונתקנים בה – זה **העיבור**.

They [the lights and the *Kelim*] come out [466] to their positions; this is the birth (Leidah).

יצאו למקומם - זו היא **לידה**.

When the lower *Partsuf* [467] dresses the higher *Partsuf* and grows to his size; this is the

הלביש תחתון לעליון והגיע לשיעורו - זה **הגדלות**.

---

461 Union
462 Feminine waters
463 *Mayim Duchrin* (masculine waters)
464 *Mayim Nukvin* and *Mayim Duchrin*
465 In her *Yesod*
466 After the time of the gestation, their details are distinct
467 Now the lights and *Kelim* are arranged as a *Partsuf*

growth (*Gadlut*).

At first he suckles from the upper *Partsuf* (to gather strength), as needed for his growth, and once grown and clothed, he becomes independent.

יונק מתחלה - שהוא צריך לעליונו.
השלים והלביש - עושה את שלו.

c) The ascent of the Malkin[468] [from *Beriah* to *Atsilut*] is of forty days:
Ten days: *'Hesed* and *Netsah*, to *Netsah* of *Atsilut*.
Ten days: *Da'at* and *Tiferet*, to his *Yesod*[469].
Ten days: *Gevurah* and *Hod*, to his *Hod*[470].
Ten days: *Yesod* and *Mal'hut*, to his *Mal'hut*[471].

ג. עליתם של מלכים ארבעים יום.
כיצד ?
עשרה ימים חסד ונצח לנצחו של אצילות.
ועשרה - דעת ותפארת ליסודו.
עשרה - גבורה והוד להודו.
ועשרה - יסוד ומלכות למלכותו.

d) *'Atik* is repaired by *D'uN*[472]. His *MaH* is his front masculine side, his *BaN*; his rear feminine side. The face of *MaH* his front,

ד. נתקן עתיק דו"נ.
מ"ה שלו - זכר לפניו,
וב"ן שלו - נוק' לאחוריו.
פני מ"ה לפניו, ופני ב"ן לאחוריו.
נמצא עתיק כולו פנים.

---

[468] The *Kelim* of *Z'aT* that broke
[469] Of *Atsilut*
[470] Of *Atsilut*
[471] Of *Atsilut*
[472] By the zivoug of higher than him (*'AV* and *SaG* of *Adam Kadmon*)

the face of *BaN* his rear[473];
thus, *'Atik* is all face.
Arikh Anpin is repaired by
D'uN; masculine [474] on his
right, feminine [475] on his
left.
The *Tikun* of *Arikh Anpin* is
from the *Zivug* of *'Atik*. The
Tikun of *'Atik* is from the
Zivug of higher than him.

e) By the *Zivug* of *Arikh
Anpin*; *Abah* and *Imah* are
arranged, this one
masculine and this one
feminine, and from their
Zivug[476]; *Z'A* and *Nukvah*
are built. The *Yesod* of *'Atik*
ends in the chest[477] of *Arikh
Anpin*,[478] the *'Hasadim* and
Gevurot are revealed from
it[479].

נתקן אריך דו"נ,
הזכר בימינו והנוקבא בשמאלו.
תיקונו של א"א מזיווגו של עתיק.
תיקונו של עתיק מזיווג עליון
ממנו.

ה. מזיווגו של א"א נתקנים או"א,
זה זכר וזה נקבה,
ומזיווגם - זו"ן.
יסודו של עתיק כלה בחזהו של
א"א,
וחו"ג מתגלים ממנו.

---

[473] His *MaH* and *BaN* are back to back
[474] His aspect of *MaH*
[475] His aspect of *BaN*
[476] Of *Abah* and *Imah*
[477] *Tiferet*
[478] According to the *Hishtalshelout* (development) but not for the clothing,
where it is in the *Yesod* of *Arich Anpin*
[479] *Yesod* of *Atik*

The *Gevurot* came out[480] first, being pushed out by the *'Hasadim;* they surrounded *Yesod* [of *'Atik*] on all sides. The *'Hasadim* came out; their halves[481] to the right, and pushed all the *Gevurot* to its left [of *Yesod*]. Their halves[482] descended, from the chest and lower, and the *'Hasadim* also descended to appease them. Therefore, there are two and a half *'Hasadim* revealed and two and a half covered, which are spreading their lights[483] to the outside.

From the *'Hasadim, Abah* and *Israel Saba* came out to the right of *Arikh*, and from the *Gevurot, Imah* and *Tevunah* came out to his left. *Imah* and *Tevunah*; the legs of one [*Imah*] in the

יצאו הגבורות ראשונה מפני
דוחקם של חסדים,
סבבו את היסוד לכל רוח.
יצאו החסדים חצים לימין,
ודחו את הגבורות כולם לשמאלו.
ירדו חצים מן החזה ולמטה,
והחסדים יורדים כנגדם למתקם.
נמצאו:
ב' חסדים וחצי מגולים,
וב' חסדים וחצי מכוסים,
מוציאים הארתם לחוץ.

יצאו מן החסדים אבא וישראל
סבא לימין של אריך,
ומן הגבורות אימא ותבונה
לשמאלו.
אימא ותבונה - רגליה של זו
בראשה של זו;
מה שאינו כן אבא וי"ס.

---

[480] From the *Yesod* of *Atik*
[481] Two and a half
[482] Two and a half of the *Gevurot*
[483] From *Yesod* they project though a veil
[484] Which are not attached

head of the other [*Tevunah*], it is not the same for *Abah* and *Israel Saba*[484], because two halves of *Gevurot* are revealed as one, while half of *'Hasadim* are covered in *Yesod*.

ששני חצאיהם של גבורות מגולים כאחד,
וחצים של חסדים מכוסים ביסוד.

f) *Abah* and *Imah* are the two *Mo'hin*[485] [brains] of *Atsilut;* they dress the two arms [*'Hesed* and *Gevurah*] of *Arikh*. They are constructed from *MaH* and *BaN,* and built[486] by the lights of *Arikh*.

ו. אוי״א - שני מוחותיו של אצילות מלבישים זרועותיו של אי״א.
בנינם ממי״ה ובי״ן,
ותיקוניהם מאורותיו של אריך.

From the three parts[487] of the arms [*'Hesed* and *Gevurah* of *Arikh*], to their *HBD* [of *Abah* and *Imah*], and from *Tiferet* [of *Arikh*], to the rest of their body [of *Abah* and *Imah*]. From the first three parts of *HGT* [of *Arikh*], to make their *Mo'hin* as one, from the

מג׳ פרקיהם של זרועות לחב״ד שלהם,
ומת״ת לשאר כל גופם.
ומג׳ פרקים ראשונים של חג״ת לעשות מוחותיהם כאחד,
מפרקים שניים לחג״ת שלהם,
מפרקים שלישיים לנה״י שלהם.

---

[485] *'Hokhma* and *Binah*
[486] Their actions are influenced by the lights of *Arich*
[487] *'Hesed* and *Gevurah* have three parts each
[488] The first parts

second parts to make their *HGT*, and from the third parts; their *NHY*.

The first parts of the right [arm] is clothed in the head of *Abah*, at the same level[488]; the left [arm] is clothed in *Imah*, the second [parts are clothed] in their *HGT*, and the third [parts] in their *NHY*.

פרקו הראשון של ימין מתלבש
בראשו של אבא,
כנגדו בשמאל באימא,
שני לו בחג״ת של זה וזה, שלישי
לו בנה״י,

Tiferet [of *Arikh*] is covered under them, until the chest.

והת״ת נכסה תחתיהן מאליו עד
החזה.

g) *Abah* and *Imah,* have *MaH* and *BaN* in them. When they[489] joined, *Abah* gave his *BaN* to *Imah,* and took her *MaH* for himself. Two *MaH* on the right: *Abah* and *Israel Saba* Two *BaN* on the left: *Imah* and *Tevunah.*

ז. או״א - מ״ה וב״ן בשניהם.
נתחברו זה בזה,
נתן אבא ב״ן שלו לאימא,
ונטל מ״ה שלה לעצמו.
שני מ״ה בימין - אבא ויש״ס,
שני ב״ן בשמאל - אימא ותבונה

---

[489] *Abah* and *Imah*

h) *ISOT*[490] how [are they constructed]? The *Malhuts* of *Abah* and *Imah* become distinct *Partsufim*, half of their *Tiferet,* and *NHY* [of *Abah* and *Imah*] dress inside of them[491], as their *Mo'hin.*

Abah and *Imah* are completed again; from there and up[492]. *Abah* and *Imah* are at the level of the chest of *Arikh*, *ISOT* is at [the level of] his navel.

Abah and *Israel Saba*, [as] *Imah* and *Tevunah* are sometimes two [493], and sometimes one [494]; when they are joined one to the other.

i) The *Mo'hin* of *Z'A* are from *Abah* and *Imah*, they

ח. ישסו״ת כיצד ?
מלכותם של או״א נעשית פרצוף לעצמה,
וחצי ת״ת ונה״י שלהם מלובשים מוחים בתוכם.

חזרו או״א להשתלם משם ולמעלה.
נמצאו :
או״א כלים בחזה של אי״א,
יסו״ת בטבור שלו.

אבא ויי״ס אימא ותבונה –
פעמים שנים, פעמים אחד –
שהם מתחברים זה בזה.

ט. מוחין של ז״א מאו״א,
מלובשים בכלים שלהם, זהו

---

[490] *Israel Saba* and *Tevunah*
[491] *Mal'hut - ISOT*
[492] With new *NHY*
[493] Two separate *Partsufim*
[494] *Partsuf*

are clothed in their *Kelim*[495], this is the צלמ.

How?

The *Mal'hut* of the superior [*Partsuf*] is the interiority of the lower; the *Malhuts* of *Abah* and *Imah* are in *Z'A*. Her *NHY*[496] enter in him, her nine parts[497] in his nine limbs [of *Z'A*]; this is the צ. Her first seven [*KHBD HGT* of *Tevunah*] are encircling him on the outside; this is his ל מ.

j) [When] *Abah* and *Imah*, [are separated from] *ISOT* [which] are two[498], *Z'A* is lower than all, and his *Mo'hin* are from *ISOT*.

[When] Their Malhuts [499] are his צלמ, this corresponds to *ISOT* 2. From their chest [of *ISOT* 2] and down [*NHY*], *Mo'hin*

הצל״ם.

כיצד ?

מלכותו של עליון פנימיות בתחתון
—
מלכותם של או״א בז״א.
נה״י שבה נכנסים בתוכו,
ט׳ פירקיהן בט׳ איבריו, זה צ׳.
ושבע ראשונות שלה מקיפים עליו
מבחוץ –
ל׳ מ׳ שלו.

י. או״א ישסו״ת - שנים,
ז״א למטה מכולם, מוחיו מיסו״ת.

מלכות שלהם צלם שלו,
אלו יסו״ת שניים.
מן החזה שלהם ולמטה ניתן לו
למוחין.
ונעשים כנגדם נה״י חדשים

---

[495] Of *ISOT,* or *Abah* and *Imah*; depending on the state of growth of *Z'A*

[496] Of *Tevunah*

[497] *NHY* of *Tevunah* have three parts each

[498] *ISOT* 1 and *ISOT* 2

[499] Of *ISOT*

are given to him [*Z'A*]. New *NHY* are made for them[500], extending and going down his back to the level of his chest, like a mother covering her young.

לעצמם,
משתלשלים ויורדים מאחוריו עד כנגד החזה,
כאם זו שרובצת על בניה.

From the chest [of *ISOT* 2] and up[501], this is his למ, corresponding to the first growth. [*Gadlut* 1]

מן החזה ולמעלה : ל׳ מ׳ שלו,
זה גדלות ראשון.

k) [When] They [*Abah, Imah,* and *ISOT*] are one, and *Z'A* is under them, his *Mo'hin* are [directly] from *Abah* and *Imah*, and their Malhuts[502] are his צלמ; there is then only one *ISOT*.

יא. נעשו אחד,
וז״א למטה מהם, מוחיו מאוי״א,
מלכות שלהם צל״ם שלו,
אין כאן ישסו״ת אלא אחת.

From the chest and down[503] are his צ, the rest[504] are his למ; corresponding to the second growth. [*Gadlut* 2]

מן החזה ולמטה - צ׳ שלו,
והשאר - ל׳ מ׳.
הרי זה גדלות שני.

---

[500] *ISOT* 2
[501] The *Sephirot* on top of *NHY* of *Tevunah* are his למ (his exterior *Mo'hin*)
[502] Of *Abah* and *Imah*
[503] *NHY*
[504] The *Sephirot* on top of *NHY*

l) The *Zivug* of *Abah* and *Imah* is constant, but the one of *ISOT* is occasional. The *Zivug* for the liveliness of the worlds is constant, but the one of the *Mo'hin* is occasional

יב. זיווג של או״א תדירי,
ושל יסו״ת - לפרקים.
זיווג חיות העולמות - תדירי,
ושל מוחים - בזמנם.

Fourth chapter

a) *Z'A* integrates the six edges [505] of the world [of *Atsilut*], and *Nukvah* is its *Mal'hut* [506] . *Arikh Anpin* folded his legs[507] and drew them on his *HGT*. The *Kelim* of *Z'A* ascended after them and clothed them[508]. The same as their shape in *Arikh Anpin*, is their shape in *Z'A*; three on top of three, and *Mal'hut* fourth after them.

Arikh Anpin took them[509], sorted them, and then by his *Zivug* [with his *Nukvah*], took them out. *Abah* and *Imah* took them [510] , and repaired them definitely; in three days, forty days, three months and two gestations.

פרק רביעי

א. ז״א - שש קצותיו של עולם,
ונוק׳ - מלכות שלו.
קפל א״א את רגליו והעלם על
חג״ת שלו.
עלו כליו של ז״א אחריהן
והלבישום.
כצורתן בא״א צורתם בז״א –
שלש על גבי שלש,
ומלכות - רביעית אחריהם.

נטלם א״א ובררם, והוציאם
בזיווגו.
נטלום או״א ותקנום לגמרי :
בג׳ ימים, ובמ׳ יום, בג׳ חדשים,
ובג׳ עיבורים.

---

[505] *Abah* and *Imah* are the *Mo'hin*
[506] Of *Atsilut*
[507] His *NHY*
[508] The *NHY* of *Arich Anpin*
[509] From *NHY* of *Atsilut*
[510] The *Kelim*

b) In three days, how? Those are the three days of *Klita* (insemination): the first day, *Abah* repaired the right in them [*Z'uN*], the second day, *Imah* repaired the left in them, the third day, *Abah* gave of himself[511] to *Imah* and they were joined [the right and the left side].

There are three *Miluim*[512] [of sparks]: The *Miluy* of *MaH* is nineteen, the *Miluy* of *SaG* is thirty seven, and the *Miluy* of *'AV* is forty six.

For the *Tikun* of *Z'A*, six of the nineteen [sparks] entered on the first day, six on the second, and seven on the third. Why six[513]? Because the lines [columns] of *Z'A* are repaired by them. On the third [day], one

ב. ג׳ ימים כיצד ?
אלו ג׳ ימים של קליטה .
יום א׳ : תיקן אבא את הימין
שבהם.
יום ב׳: אימא את השמאל שבהם.
יום ג׳: נתן אבא את שלו באימא,
ונתחברו אלה באלה.

ג׳ מילוים הם :
מילויו של מ״ה - י״ט. ושל ס״ג -
ל״ז, ושל ע״ב - מ״ו.

תיקונו של ז״א –
ו׳ מיי״ט נכנסים ביום ראשון, ו׳
בב׳, ז׳ בג׳.
למה ו׳ ? שקויו של ז״א נתקנים
בהם.
ובשלישי אחד יותר מפני חבורם
של אורות.

---

[511] Of what he repaired
[512] In the sense of filling. Each name of *ASMB* less the initials of *YKVK* (26)
[513] After it is only one spark a day
[514] With the three first days
[515] This makes a total of 86 days (close to 3 lunar months)

more because of the joining of the lights [of the right and left columns].

Thirty seven [sparks] in thirty seven days, this makes forty days [514], the infant is formed by the light of *Imah*, forty six [sparks], in forty six days[515], as the three months needed to distinguish the fetus.

c) The construction of *Z'A* [includes]: *Kelim*, sparks, and lights. The *Kelim* that broke, the sparks that descended, and the lights that departed [went back up when the *Kelim* broke]. They came back and repaired one another[516] in three gestations[517]; one of seven months[518], one of nine[519], and one of twelve[520] months.

לי"ז בלי"ז ימים - הרי מ' יום.
נוצר הולד באורה של אימא,
מ"ו במ"ו ימים ; כמשלוש חדשים
—
זמן היכרו של עובר

ג. בנינו של ז"א —
כלים וניצוצות ואורות :
כלים שנשברו,
ניצוצות שירדו,
אורות שנסתלקו.
חוזרים ונתקנים זה בזה בג'
עיבורים —
של ז' חדשים, ושל ט', ושל י"ב.

---

[516] By being together, the damage was their separation from each other
[517] One for the sparks, one for the *Kelim* and one for the lights
[518] For the lights
[519] For the sparks
[520] For the *Kelim*
[521] Of *Z'A*

Imah and *Tevunah* joined as one, and there are three levels of *Yesod* in them: *Yesod* of *Imah*, *Yesod* of *Tevunah,* and the place of the cutting when they are separated and cut from each other.

His *Kelim*[521] are repaired by *Yesod* of *Tevunah*, his sparks, at the place of the cutting, and his lights, by *Yesod* of *Binah* [*Imah*]. In the lower world, there are also three sections[522].

d) The body of *Z'A* is composed of ten *Sephirot*. Seven *Sephirot* [523] were established in seven month[524], and three[525] in the twenty four month of the suckling; eight month each. Seven [months] which are nine, because *Da'at* divides

אימא ותבונה מתחברים כאחד,

וג' מקומות של יסוד יש בהם:

יסודה של אימא,

ויסודה של תבונה,

ומקום החתך - כשהן מתפרדות

נחתכות זו מזו.

נתקנים כליו ביסודה של תבונה,

ניצוציו במקום החתך,

אורותיו ביסודה של בינה.

כנגדם למטה ג' מדורות.

ד. גופו של ז"א עשר ספירות.

נתבררו ז' ספירות בז' חדשים,

וג' ספירות בכ"ד חדשים של

יניקה,

ח' חדשים לאחת.

ז' שהם ט',

שהדעת מתחלק לחסדים וגבורות.

---

[522] In the woman (Nidah, 31, 1)
[523] *Keter, 'Hokhma, Binah, 'Hesed, Gevurah, Tiferet, Netsah*
[524] Of the gestation
[525] *Hod, Yesod* and *Mal'hut*

in 'Hasadim and Gevurot.

e) They are three Kelim: NHY is the first Keli, [the keli of] HGT is in his interior, and [the keli of] HBD is in the interior of HGT.

ה. ג׳ כלים הם: נה״י כלי א׳, פנימי לו חג״ת, פנימי לו חב״ד.

There are three Neshamot[526] in them: Nefesh in NHY, Rua'h in HGT, and Neshama in HBD. When are they repaired? During the gestation, the suckling, and [when they receive] the Mo'hin[527].

וג׳ נשמות בתוכם – נפש בנה״י, רוח בחג״ת, נשמה בחב״ד. אימתי הם נתקנים ? בעיבור יניקה ומוחין.

f) NHY[528] in the gestation how[529]? Its NHY[530] and its HGT[531] are its exteriority, HBD[532] is the Nefesh in them.

ו. כיצד נה״י בעיבור ? נה״י וחג״ת שלו - חיצוניות, וחב״ד - נפש בתוכם.

---

[526] Nefesh, Rua'h and Neshama
[527] When they are in Z'A
[528] Which is the exterior Keli
[529] How is it repaired?
[530] NHY of NHY
[531] HGT of NHY
[532] HBD of NHY

HGT[533] [is repaired] in the suckling; its *NHY*[534] and its *HGT*[535] are its exteriority, *HBD*[536] is the *Rua'h* in them.

HBD[537] [is repaired] in the growth, these are all the *HGT* that ascend and become *HBD*, the *NHY* take their place[538], and new *NHY* are renewed lower for them[539].

HBD spreads down on all; this corresponds to the *Neshama* [soul] which contains *Nefesh*, *Rua'h*, *Neshama*, *'Hayah* and *Ye'hidah*. *NRN*[540] are the interiority, *'Hayah* and *Ye'hidah* are their encircling, and all the *Kelim* are exteriority to them

חג״ת ביניקה ?
נה״י וחג״ת : חיצוניות,
וחב״ד רוח בתוכם.

חב״ד בגדלות ?
אלו חג״ת שעולים ונעשים חב״ד,
ונה״י במקומם,
ונה״י אחרים מתחדשים להם
למטה.

חב״ד יורדים בכולם,
זהו נשמה, שבה נרנח״י.
נר״ן - פנימים, ח״י – מקיפים
להם.

חזרו כל הכלים חיצוניות לגבה.

---

[533] Which is the intermediate *Keli*
[534] *NHY* of *HGT*
[535] *HGT* of *HGT*
[536] *HBD* of *HGT*
[537] Which is the interior *Keli*
[538] Of *HGT*
[539] To replace the *NHY* that became *HGT*
[540] *Nefesh*, *Rua'h* and *Neshama*
[541] Each one of the three aspects has its own three aspects

[*HBD*].

Three composed of three[541]:
NHY HGT HBD in *NHY*,
[the three aspects of the exterior *Keli*]
NHY HGT HBD in *HGT*,
[the three aspects of the intermediate *Keli*]
NHY HGT HBD in *HBD*,
[the three aspects of the interior *Keli*]
NRN of the growth, inside of all.
As it is in man: flesh, veins, bones, and *NRN* in them.

ג' של ג':

נה"י חג"ת חב"ד - בנה"י,

נה"י חג"ת חב"ד - בחג"ת,

נה"י חג"ת חב"ד - בחב"ד.

ונר"נ של גדלות בתוך כולם.

כנגדם באדם –
בשר וגידים ועצמות, ונר"נ בתוכם.

g) [During the growth] All the [*Kelim* of the aspects of] *NHY* become *NHY*, all the *HGT* [become] *HGT*, and all the *HBD* [become] *HBD*.
HBD of *NHY*: bones[542],
HBD of *HGT*: veins,
HBD of *HBD*: *Mo'hin*,
As in the body of man[543]: bones, veins, cranium and

ז. כל הנה"י נעשים נה"י,

וכל חג"ת - חג"ת,

וכל חב"ד - חב"ד.

חב"ד שמנה"י - עצמות,

חב"ד מחג"ת - קרומות,

חב"ד מחב"ד - מוחין;

שכן בגופו של אדם

עצמות קרומות ומוחין,

ונשמה בתוכם.

---

[542] Cranium

Neshama inside of them.

The exteriors are the *NHY* and *HGT*, the interiors are the *HBD*. As for man: body and soul (*Neshama*).

חזרו כל החיצוניות - נה"י וחג"ת, וכל הפנימיות - חב"ד להם. כנגדם באדם - גוף ונשמה.

The *Kelim* divided as interiors and exteriors; the *Neshama* in them is lights and sparks. From all of these elements, *Z'A* is constructed.

נחלקו הכלים לפנימי וחיצון, ונשמה בתוכם - אורות וניצוצות. בנינו של ז"א משוכלל מכל אלו.

h) There are four gestations [for *Z'A*], two for [the making of the levels of] its exteriors [544], and two for [the making of the levels of] its interiors [545] - gestation for its six lower [*Sephirot*], and gestation for its *Mo'hin*.

ח. ד' עיבורים הם: ב' בחיצוניותו, וב' בפנימיותו – עיבור דו"ק, ועיבור דמוחין.

The first gestation [for its six lower *Sephirot*] is of twelve months, the second [for its *Mo'hin*] is of nine

עיבור ראשון י"ב חדשים, שני לו ט' בחיצוניות. כנגדם בפנימיות - של ט', ושל ז'.

[months]; this is for its exteriors. It is the same for its interiors; nine [months for its six lower *Sephirot*], and seven [months for its *Mo'hin*].

i) The [period of the] suckling is twenty four month; [546] it is for the clarification of *Hod, Yesod* and *Mal'hut*. From here to growth, it will take eleven years and one day. How? Seven parts of *NHY* of *Tevunah* [enter *Z'A*] in seven years, and its crown[547]; in one day. From her [548] , come out the revealed *'Hasadim,* from the chest [of *Z'A*] and downward.

They [the *'Hasadim*] come down to group in *Yesod* [of *Z'A*], and return upwards on their columns [*Netsah* and *Hod*], until they ascend in

ט. היניקה כ"ד חדשים .
בירורם של הי"מ.
ממנה לגדלות יי"א שנה ויום א'.
כיצד ?
ז' פרקיהם של נה"יי דתבונה בז'
שנים,
ועטרה שלה ביום א',
שבו יוצאים החסדים מגולים מן
החזה ולמטה.

יורדים ונכללים ביסוד,
וחוזרים בקוויהם מלמטה למעלה
עד שעולים בכל שש קצותיו.

---

[546] Eight months each
[547] Of *Yesod*
[548] The crown of *Yesod*

all the six edges [of *Z'A*].

Five *Gevurot* come down afterwards, and are sweetened [appeased] in *Yesod* [of *Z'A*]; two and a half in the descent, the rest, [are sweetened] by the *'Hasadim* returning upwards.

ה' גבורות יורדות אחריהן
ונמתקים ביסוד,
ב' וחצי בירידה,
והשאר בחזירתם של חסדים
עולים ומתמתקים אתם.

The *'Hasadim* are the growth for *Z'A*, the *Gevurot* are the growth for *Nukvah*. The guidance of the masculine is of the right, the one of the feminine is of the left.

החסדים - גידולו של זעיר.
והגבורות - גידולה של נוק'.
שהנהגתו של זכר לימין, ושל נוק'
לשמאל.

j) The *'Hasadim* returned[549] to *'Hesed* and *Gevurah* [of *Z'A*], they[550] augmented and doubled[551]. Each one is now of six thirds; three stayed in their place[552], two went up from *'Hesed* to *'Hokhma*,

י. חזרו החסדים לחסד ולגבורה,
והגדילום, והם נכפלים.
נמצאו כל אחד ו' שלישים .
ג' נשארים במקומם,
ב' מחסד עולים לחכמה,
וב' מגבורה לבינה,
והשלישי שבשניהם לימין ושמאל

---

[549] From *Yesod* of *Z'A*
[550] The *'Hasadim*
[551] From three thirds to six thirds
[552] In the *Kelim* of *'Hesed* and *Gevurah*
[553] The first third of *Tiferet* which is hidden or covered

two from *Gevurah* to
Binah, one third [shared] in
each ['*Hesed* and *Gevurah*,
went up] on the right and
left of *Da'at*.

שבדעת.

Two of the thirds of *Tiferet*
doubled and became four,
two [stayed] in their place,
one ascended to *Keter* of
Nukvah, one went up to the
one that is covered[553], and
doubled [in size]. One
[covered] remained in his
place, and one[554] came up
with him[555] until *Keter* [of
Z'A].

נכפלו ב׳ שלישיו של ת״ת ונעשו ד׳
ב׳ למקומם,
א׳ לכתר נוק׳,
וא׳ עולה למכוסה, ומכפילו.
נשאר א׳ במקומו,
וא׳ מעלהו עמו עד הכתר.

Two Kings [*Zeir Anpin* and
Nukvah] are sharing the
same crown; *Z'A* completes
himself with his.

נמצאו שני מלכים משתמשים
בכתר אחד.
וז״א נשלם בשלו.

The ascent of the '*Hasadim*
to *HBD* is of three years,
and one year to *Keter*,
which is above them.

עליתם של חסדים בחב״ד ג׳ שנים,
ושנה, לכתר ששורה על גביהם.

This is the time necessary

יומם של חסדים עולים לכתר.

---

[554] Of the uncovered thirds
[555] Covered third

for the ascent of the *Hasadim* to *Keter*. Thirteen years and one day, this is the period of growth.

והרי י"ג שנים ויום א',
זה הגדלות.

k) On top[556] of צ, there are ל מ, which are encircling [Z'A]. The time[557] [for them to arrive] is two years; these are from *Imah*.

יא. למעלה מצי - לי מי מקיפין.
זמנם שתי שנים,
אלו מאימא.

The interior [Mo'hin] of *Abah*; [take] three years [to enter in Z'A], and two years for his encircling; this is the completion of the beard.

פנימים דאבא ג' שנים.
ובי שנים למקיפין,
הרי זה מלוי זקן.

l) [When Z'A receives its Mo'hin] From *Tevunah*, there are states of infancy and growth [for Z'A], a first state of infancy, and a first state of growth. Similarly, from *Imah*; there is a second state of infancy, and a second state of growth.

יב. בתבונה - קטנות וגדלות:
קטנות ראשונה, וגדלות ראשונה.
כנגדם באיי - קטנות וגדלות שנייה.

---

[556] On top of צ which represents the interior *Mo'hin*, there are *Mo'hin* encircling by the outside

[557] For the exterior *Mo'hin*

[558] The entrance, the propagation (of the *Mo'hin* of *Tevunah*).

[559] The *Mo'hin* from *Imah*

As it is for the first[558], it is
for the second[559]. The first
Mo'hin are from lower
[*Tevunah*], the seconds, are
from higher [*Imah*].

כעניינו בראשונה עניינו בשנייה.
שמוחין הראשונים מלמטה,
והשניים מלמעלה.

Fifth chapter

a) The [first] state of *Nukvah* corresponds to one dot; the seventh of six [*Sephirot*]. When *Z'A* ascends, she ascends with him; during the gestation, the suckling and the growth.

b) [During the gestation] The Six edges [of *Z'A*], are three on three [560], and *Mal'hut* is fourth after them on *Yesod* [of *Z'A*].

[During the suckling] *NHY* [561] descended, and *HGT* [562] were revealed. *Mal'hut* stayed attached to the back of *Tiferet*.

[During the growth] *HGT* ascended and became *HBD*, *Mal'hut* ascended and was rooted in *Da'at*[563].

פרק חמישי

א. קביעותה של נוק' – נקודה אחת, שביעית לששה. עלה הז"א, ועלתה אחריו בעיבור וביניקה ובגדלות.

ב. וי"ק תלת גו תלת, והמלכות רביעית אחריהן על היסוד.

ירדו נה"י ונתגלו חג"ת, נשארה המלכות דבוקה בת"ת מאחוריו.

עלו חג"ת ונעשו חב"ד, עלתה המלכות ונשרשה בדעת.

---

[560] *NHY* fold on *HGT*
[561] Of *Z'A*
[562] Of *Z'A*
[563] Of *Z'A*

c) She [*Nukvah*] descends [from *Da'at*] to be constructed, she is built by the rears of his *NHY* [of *Z'A*].

Tiferet[564] [of *Z'A*] in *Keter* [of *Nukvah*], *Netsah* and *Hod* [of *Z'A*] in *'Hokhma* and *Binah* [of *Nukvah*], *Yesod* [of *Z'A*] in *Da'at* [of *Nukvah*] between her shoulders, those are the first parts [565] [of *NHY*], the remainder[566] in the rest of her body [of *Nukvah*].

Eight years for eight parts [567], the masculine *Yesod* [of *Z'A*] is two parts long; he ends at the end of her *Tiferet*[568], from there, the *Gevurot* descend from him to her *Yesod*[569]; [this is done] in one day.

ג. יורדת להבנות –
בנינה מנה״י שלו מאחוריהם.
ת״ת בכתר, נו״ה בחו״ב, יסוד
בדעת שבין כתפיה.
אלו פרקים ראשונים,
והשאר בשאר גופה.

ח׳ שנים לח׳ פרקיהם,
שיסודו של זכר ארוך ב׳ פרקים.
נמצא כלה בסוף ת״ת שלה,
שמשם יורדות הגבורות ממנו
ליסוד שלה ביום א׳.

---

[564] The two lower thirds of *Tiferet*
[565] Of three parts
[566] Of the parts of *NHY*
[567] Three parts of *Netsah*, three parts of *Hod* and two parts of *Yesod*
[568] Of *Nukvah*
[569] Of *Nukvah*

They [the *Gevurot*] return upwards [in *Nukvah*] from *Yesod* to *Tiferet;* one year, from it [*Tiferet*] to *Da'at;* one year, one year for [the construction of] her *Keter*, and from *Da'at* to *Keter;* one year. These are [make] the twelve years and one day; because the *Nukvah* precedes the masculine [by one year].

חוזרים מלמטה למעלה :
מיסוד לת״ת שנה א׳,
ממנה לדעת שנה א׳,
שנה אחת לכתר שלה,
מדעת לכתר שנה א׳.
אלו י״ב שנים ויום א׳,
שהנוק׳ מקדמת לזכר.

Z'uN were attached by their backs, about them he says: "Back and front you have restricted me, and laid your hand upon me" (Tehilim 139, 5)

נמצאו דו״ן מדובקים מאחוריהם,
ועליהם הוא אומר (תהלים קלט,
ה) :
"אחור וקדם צרתני".

d) *Imah*[570] comes out from *Z'A*, his *Mo'hin* [571] are contained in her [in *NHY* of *Imah*], and *NHY* of *Abah* are clothed in her [in *NHY* of *Imah*].

ד. יוצאת אימא מז״א, ומוחיו
בתוכה.
ונה״י אבא מלובשים בה.

---

[570] Her *NHY*
[571] Of *Z'A*

They enter [572] to build *Nukvah*, and she is appeased [573] by them. *'Hesed* [of *Imah*] spreads in *Z'A* who pushes out the *Gevurot* from his rears, they are given through them[574] to *Nukvah*, and she separates from him [*Z'A*].

נכנסים ובונים את הנוק׳ מתוקנת על ידיהם.
וחסד נמשך לז״א שדוחה הגבורות שבאחוריו,
וניתנים על ידיהם לנוק׳,
וננסרה ממנו.

Nukvah is built from the left [575], and *Z'A* from the right [576]. They find themselves facing each other, and she is built[577] in front of him.

נמצא:
נוק׳ בנויה לשמאל,
וז״א לימין.
חוזרים זה נגד זה ונבנית לפניו.

On them, it is written:
"And the rib, which the Lord G-d had taken from man, made He a woman, and brought her to the man" (Bereshit, 2, 22)

עליהם הוא אומר (בראשית ב, כב):
"ויבן ה׳ אלהים את הצלע ויביאה אל האדם".

---

[572] In *Nukvah*
[573] The *Gevurot* given by *Abah* and *Imah* to her are more appeased than the ones given by *Z'A*
[574] The rears of *Z'A*
[575] From the aspects of the *Gevurot*
[576] From the aspects of the *'Hasadim*
[577] Being separated from him

e) The construction of a *Partsuf* is done by the twenty two letters. Twenty two letters are given from *Z'A* to *Nukvah*; they integrate in her *Yesod*, and [she also receives] מנצפך (the five final letters) corresponding to the *Gevurot* and containing *M'N*[578].

Twenty two more letters are given to her[579] from *Imah*, but not through *Z'A*, and also מנצפך containing *M'N*.

The twenty two letters [make] one *Dalet* (ד) with an axis; They are two *Dalet* [580] with two axis, which make one **ם**; this is the *Keli*.

Twenty two letters from *Imah* are like one[581]; one

ה. בנינו של פרצוף בכ״ב אותיות. כ״ב אותיות לנוק׳ מז״א, נכללים ביסודה, ומנצפ״ך גבורות מ״ן בתוכם.

וכ״ב אחרות ניתנות לה מאימא שלא על ידו, ומנצפ״ך מ״ן בתוכם.

כ״ב אותיות דלת וציר נמצאו שתי דלתות ושני צירים שהם ם אחת, זה הכלי.

כ״ב אותיות מאימא נכללים כאחד,

---

[578] *Mayim Nukvin*
[579] To *Nukvah*
[580] One from *Z'A* and one from *Imah*
[581] One letter with the shape of a *Dalet* (ד)

month for the twenty two letters and five months for the five מנצפך; that makes the six months corresponding to the period between the young girl and puberty.

חודש לכ״ב אותיות,

והי חדשים להי של מנצפ"ך –

ששה חדשים שבין נערות לבגרות.

f) There is a screen (divider) that separates one world from another. From this screen, the ten *Sephirot* of the lower world come out from the ten *Sephirot* of the higher world.

All the worlds are equal[582], but the quintessence of the higher is superior.

Beriah came out [583] ; the separate beings came to be[584]. The *Neshamot* of the Tsadikim are from *Beriah*, below it, is *Yetsirah;* from there the angels come out, and below it, is *'Asiah;* from there the physical emerges.

ו. ופרגוד בין עולם לעולם,

שממנו יוצאין עשר ספירות של תחתון

מעשר ספירותיו של עליון.

כל העולמות שוים,

אלא שכחם של עליונים יפה.

יצתה **בריאה**, התחילו הנפרדים.

נשמותיהם של צדיקים מבריאה,

למטה ממנו **יצירה**, שמשם מלאכים.

למטה ממנה **עשיה**, שמשם גשמים.

---

[582] They all contain 10 *Sephirot* and five *Partsufim*
[583] From the world of *Atsilut*
[584] Started to exist
[585] *Tetragamon* (יקוק)

The total of the worlds is four; upon them, the four letters of the Name[585] B'H, govern. י in *Atsilut;* by it, all the repaired levels are put in order. ה descends from it (*Atsilut*) to *Beriah,* and guides it. ו to *Yetsirah,* and ה to *'Asiah.*

In parallel (to these four worlds) there are in this world: דומם, (mineral), צומח (vegetal), חי (animal), and מדבר (man), As it is written:

"Every one who is called by My Name; for I have created him for My glory, I have formed him; yes, I have made him" (Isaiah, 43,7)

כללם של עולמות ד',
שבהם שולטים ד' אותיות של
השם ב"ה.
י' **באצילות**, שבו כל מדרגותיו
נסדרות בתיקונם.
וה' יורדת ממנו **לבריאה**,
ומנהיגתה ; ו' **ליצירה** ; ה' **לעשיה**.

כנגדם בעולם - דצח"ם.
וכן הוא אומר (ישעיה מג, ז) :
"כל הנקרא בשמי ולכבודי
בראתיו יצרתיו אף עשיתיו".

Sixth chapter

a) The abundance of the world proceeds from the *Zivug* of *Z'uN*. There are five *Zivugim: Israel* and *Ra'hel*, *Ya'acov* and *Ra'hel*, *Israel* and *Leah*, *Ya'acov* and *Leah* from the chest up, *Ya'acov* and *Leah* from the chest down.

b) $M'D$[586] and $M'N$[587], are the essential of the *Zivug*. $M'N$ proceeds from the feminine, and $M'D$ from the masculine. There is no $M'D$ without $M'N$, and there is no $M'N$ without desire. As it is written: "And your desire shall be to your husband" (Bereshit, 3, 16).

c) [For the *Tikun*] *Nukvah* includes her ramifications[588] in her, and adorns herself

---

[586] *Mayim Duchrin* (masculine waters)
[587] *Mayim Nukvin* (feminine waters)
[588] The worlds of *Beriah*, *Yetsirah* and *'Asiah*

פרק ששי

א. שפעו של עולם מזיווגם של זו"ן.
ה' זיווגים הם .
ישראל ורחל, יעקב ורחל,
ישראל ולאה, יעקב ולאה מן החזה ולמעלה,
יעקב ולאה אף מן החזה ולמטה.

ב. מי"ד ומי"ן –
זה גופו של זיווג.
מי"ן מן הנקבה ומי"ד מך הזכר.
אין מי"ד בלא מי"ן.
ואין מי"ן בלא תשוקה.
הוא שהכתוב אומר (בראשית ג, טז) :
"ואל אישך תשוקתך".

ג. נכללת נוקבא בענפיה,
ומתקשטת בקישוטיה.
כל העולמות בי"ע - תיקוניה של

with her ornaments [589]. All the worlds, *Beriah, Yetsirah* and *'Asiah* are the *Tikun* [590] of *Nukvah*. She motivates *Z'A*, to attach and unite with her by a first and a second union.

d) On the first union, it is said:
"A woman is an unfinished vessel, and binds a covenant only with who makes her a *Keli*." (Sanhedrin 22.b).

He [*Z'A*] puts *Rua'h* in her [*Nukvah*]; this corresponds to Benyamin – *BaN*, by him [591], she brings up her children [592] ; these correspond to the *Neshamot* of the Tsadikim. Lights illuminate from her [*Nukvah*] for the guidance of the worlds; they are the

נוק'.
מתעוררת לז"א להתחבר עמו,
ומזדווג עמה –
ביאה ראשונה וביאה שניה .

ד. ביאה ראשונה –
זהו שאמרו (סנהדרין כב.): :
"האשה גולם היא
ואינה כורתת ברית אלא למי
שעשאה כלי".
נותן רוח בתוכה,
זה בנימין - ב"ן,
שבו מעלה בניה למעלה –
אלו נשמותיהן של צדיקים.
ואורות מאירים ממנה להנהגתו
של עולם,
אלו אורות של ב"ן.

---

[589] The *Hechalot*
[590] She is complete only when her branches (ramifications) attach to her
[591] *BaN*
[592] The *Neshamot* that fell during the breaking of the *Kelim*
[593] The renewal of the lights of *BaN*
[594] The renewal of the lights of *MaH*
[595] The abundance

lights of *BaN*.

All the outcomes of *BaN* depend on her [*Nukvah*]; from her 613 limbs she draws them[593], the renewal [of the lights] is from the *Ein Sof B'H*, who regenerates [their strength] in them [by a special emanation]; these are the *M'N*.

כל תולדותיו של ב״ן תלוים בה, ומתרי״ג איבריה היא ממשיכתם, מחידושו של א״ס ב״ה שהוא מחדש בהם, אלו מ״ן.

In the second union; *M'D* come down to their level [of *M'N*] from the *Yesod* of the masculine; these corresponding to the lights of *MaH*, and all the outcomes of *MaH* depend on him [*Z'A*]. From his 613 limbs he draws them[594], the renewal [of the lights] is from the *Ein Sof B'H*, who regenerates [their strength] in them [by a special emanation].

ביאה שניה – יורדים כנגדן מ״ד מיסודו של זכר ; אלו אורות של מ״ה, וכל תולדותיו של מ״ה תלוים בו. מתרי״ג איבריו הוא ממשיכם, מחידושו של א״ס שהוא מחדש בהם.

All [*M'N* and *M'D*] descend to her *Yesod* [of *Nukvah*], remain there for the time of the gestation, come out and

יורד הכל ביסודה, ויושב שם זמן עיבורו. יוצא ומתחלק לכל העולמות.

spread[595] in all the worlds.

e) *MaH* and *BaN* are the foundation of all the created[596]. By them[597], are manifested the actions of the *Ein Sof, B'H* [the Emanator][598], and the receivers[599]. They[600] are renewed by the *Zivug* of *Z'uN; MaH* from the masculine, and *BaN* from the feminine.

ה. מ״ה וב״ן - בנינם של כל הנבראים.
שבהם נראים מעשיו של א״ס ב״ה במשפיע ומקבל,
מתחדשים בזיווגם של זו״נ.
מ״ה מן הזכר, וב״ן מן הנקבה.

f) There are two unions for the *Zivug*: the kissing[601], and the *Yesodot*[602]. The kissing is in the heads, their *Zivug* is double; the *Rua'h* of the masculine is in the mouth of the feminine, and the *Rua'h* of the feminine is in the mouth of the masculine. There are then two *Ruhot* unified as one.

ו. ב׳ חיבורים לזיווג - נשיקין ויסודות.
נשיקין בראש, זיווגם כפול – רוחו של זכר בפיה של נקבה ורוחה של נקבה בפיו של זכר.
נמצאו שתי רוחות מתחברים כאחד.
זיווגם של יסודות, אחר שנתחברו, משפיע הזכר לנקבה והנקבה לעולם.

---

[596] Everything is composed of both (*MaH* and *BaN*)

[597] *MaH* and *BaN*

[598] His emanation are of the aspect of *MaH*

[599] The receivers are of the aspect of *BaN*

[600] *MaH* and *BaN*

[601] To attach the interiority of the masculine with the one of the feminine

[602] To attach the exteriority of the masculine with the one of the feminine

The *Zivug* of the *Yesodot* is done after the union [of the kisses]; the masculine bestows to the feminine, and the feminine [bestows] to the world.

Seventh chapter

a) The sum of the *Partsufim* is twelve [603], the rest [604] ; emanates from them [They are] :

Arikh Anpin and his *Nukvah*, *Abah* and *Imah*, the first *ISOT* [*Israel Sabbah, Tevunah*], the second *ISOT* [*Israel Sabbah2, Tevunah2*], *Israel, Ra'hel, Ya'acov* and *Leah*. They are clothed one inside the other[605].

b) The innermost [*Partsuf*] of these, is *Arikh Anpin* and his *Nukvah*, they make one *Partsuf;* the masculine on the right, and the feminine on the left.

Abah and *Imah* are on his arms [606] ; *Abah* is on the right, and *Imah* on the left.

פרק שביעי

א. כללם של פרצופים י״ב,
והשאר מתפשטים מהם :
א״א ונוקביה, או״א,
ישסו״ת ראשונים, ישסו״ת שניים,
ישראל ורחל, יעקב ולאה,
מתלבשים אלו בתוך אלו.

ב. פנימים מכולם - א״א ונוקביה,
פרצוף אחד הם,
שהזכר בימין והנקבה בשמאל.

ועל זרועותיו –
אבא לימין אי׳ לשמאל.
ג. פרקין בזרוע :

---

[603] Beside the *Partsuf* of *Atik*
[604] Other lights that are not complete *Partsufim*. (See Chap. 7, e.)
[605] The superior *Partsuf* dresses inside the lower to guide him
[606] Of *Arich Anpin*
[607] At the level of his throat

There are three parts of the arm: the first [part] is in their *HBD* [of *Abah* and *Imah*], the second is in their *HGT*, the third is in their *NHY*. Their *Keter* [of *Abah* and *Imah*] are in [607] his throat [*Binah* of *Arikh Anpin*], and they[608] extend downward until his navel [609]. His body [610] is covered by them [*Abah* and *Imah*] until the navel; one half by *Abah,* and one half by *Imah*.

הראשון בחב״ד, השני בחג״ת, השלישי בנה״י.
וכתרם בגרונו.
ומגיעים עד טבורו.
נמצא גופו עד הטבור מכוסה תחתיהון,
חציו מאבא וחציו מאימא

c) *ISOT* [start] from the chests of *Abah* and *Imah* and extend downward. Their *Keter* are in the chests [of *Abah* and *Imah*], the rest of their bodies [of *ISOT*] are in the parts of *NHY* [of *Abah* and *Imah*].

ג. יסו״ת מחזיהם של או״א ולמטה.
כתרם בחזה, ושאך כל גופם בפרקיהם של נה״י.

From their chests [of *ISOT*],

מחזה שלהם יסו״ת שניים כסדר

---

[608] *Abah* and *Imah*
[609] Of *Arich Anpin* (until the second third of *Tiferet*, which corresponds to the navel)
[610] Of *Arich Anpin*
[611] Until the first third of *Tiferet* and not the second, as above. Because new *NHY* are given to them when the first *NHY* become *Mo'hin* for *Z'A*

ISOT 2 follow in the same arrangement. *Abah* and *Imah* extend downward until the chest[611] of *Arikh Anpin,* and *ISOT* extend downward until his navel [of *Arikh Anpin*].

הזה.

נמצאו:

או״א כלים בחזה של אי״א,

ויסו״ת בטבורו.

When they [*NHY* of *ISOT*] enter *Z'A,* they elongate their legs [*NHY*] inside him, and reach together with him until the [lower] extremity of the world [of *Atsilut*].

כשבאים בז״א - מתארכים רגליהם בתוכו.

ומגיעים עמו עד סוף העולם

d) *Z'A* [starts] from the chests of *ISOT,* and extends down. They[612] dress inside one another, and then into him [*Z'A*].

ד. ז״א מחזיהם של יסו״ת ולמטה,

מתלבשים זה בזה, ומתלבשים בתוכו.

Ra'hel [starts] from his chest [of *Z'A*] and extends down, she is sometimes back to back, and sometimes face to face [with *Z'A*]. The *Yesod* of the

ורחל מחזה שלו ולמטה,

פעמים אבי״א ופעמים פב״פ.

יסוד של נקבות פרק וחצי,

ושל זכרים שני פרקים.

---

[612] *Israel Saba* in *Tevunah*
[613] *Tiferet* of *Z'A*
[614] *NHY* of *Imah*

feminine is one and-a- half parts [long], the one of the masculine is two parts [long].

The *Yesod* of *Abah* emerges from the *Yesod* of *Imah*, inside of *Z'A*, from the chest[613] until the *Yesod* [of *Z'A*].

נמצא יסודו של אבא יוצא מיסוד אי׳

בתוכו של ז״א מן החזה עד היסוד,

It is from him [from an illumination of *Yesod* of *Abah*], that *Ya'acov* comes out from the chest of *Z'A* and lower, in front of him. The face of *Z'A*, to the back of *Ya'acov*, sometimes he [*Ya'acov*] comes to his side, his face [of *Ya'acov*] in front of *Ra'hel*. These are the rears [*NHY*] of *Abah*, which make a *Partsuf* [*Ya'acov*], from the lights of his *Yesod* [of *Abah*].

שממנו יוצא יעקב מחזהו של ז״א ולמטה לפניו,

פני ז״א באחוריו של יעקב ;

ופעמים שהוא בא לצדו, פניו בפני רחל.

אלו אחוריים של אבא שנעשים פרצוף באור יסודו.

The rears [*NHY*] of *Imah*, [extend] from the chest of *Z'A* upwards. They[614] make a *Partsuf* with the lights of her *Yesod* [of *Imah*] - this is *Leah;* [she starts] from

אחוריים של אי׳ מן החזה של ז״א ולמעלה

נעשים פרצוף באור יסודה - זו לאה,

מן הדעת עד החזה, מאחוריו של ז״א, פניה באחוריו

Da'at [of *Z'A,* and extends] until his chest, [she is] in the back of *Z'A,* her face to his back.

e) At the back of *Ya'acov,* between him and *Z'A,* there is *Leah D'hM* [615] [דור המדבר], which is his *Nukvah.*

ה. מאחוריו של יעקב בינו ובין ז״א –לאה דור המדבר, נוק׳ שלו.

From the two sides of *Z'A,* [there are] two diagonal lights: "The *Clouds of Glory*" on his right, and "The *Manna*" on his left.

מב׳ צדדיו של ז״א שני אורות באלכסון – ענני כבוד לימינו, ומן לשמאלו.

From the two sides of *Leah D'hM,* [there are] two lights: "*The Scepter of Elokim*", and "*The Scepter of Moshe*".

מב׳ צדדיה של לאה דור המדבר – שני אורות : מטה האלהים, ומטה משה.

From the two sides of *Ya'acov,* [there are] two lights: "*Erev Rav*"[616] on his right, and "*Essav*" on his left.

Three lines of three and

ומב׳ צדדיו של יעקב – שני אורות : ערב רב לימינו, ועשו לשמאלו. נמצאו ג׳ שורות של ג׳ ג׳. כשרחל אב״א עומדים כסדר הזה.

---

[615] *Partsuf Leah*
[616] The mixed multitude

three, when *Ra'hel* is back to back, they are standing this way[617].

---

f) [There are] Eighteen [aspects of] *Leah;* they are from the Malhuts of *Abah* and *Imah*. How?

Mal'hut of *Abah* is in its place[618], *Mal'hut* of *Imah* is on its outside[619], these make two [aspects].

Mal'hut of *Abah* emerges outward from the *Mal'hut* of *Imah* and illuminates outside of her, these make three [aspects].

Mal'hut of *Imah* emerges outward, trough the body of *Z'A*, and illuminates outside of him, these make four [aspects].

The most important of all [the *Leah*], is the one on the outside, the rest [620] are subordinate to her.

ו. י"ח לאה הם ממלכיותיהם של או"א.

כיצד ؟

מלכות אבא במקומה

ומלכות אימא חוצה לה ,

הרי ב' .

מלכותו של אבא בוקע מלכותה של אי'

ומאירה חוצה לה,

הרי ג'.

מלכותה של אי' בוקעת ויוצאה,

בוקעת גופו של ז"א ומאירה חוצה לו,

הרי ד'.

עיקר שבכולם זו שבחוץ,

והשאר טפלות לה.

---

617 As described above
618 In *Mal'hut* of *Imah*
619 Of *Mal'hut* of *Abah*
620 The other aspects of *Leah*

g) The four *Mo'hin* of growth, and the four of infancy [of *Z'A*], make eight [aspects of *Leah*, that come from the Malhuts of *Abah* and *Imah*, during the infancy and growth of *Z'A*].

The ones [*Mo'hin*] of growth start to enter, while the ones of infancy have not yet finish to exit; these are eight more [aspects of *Leah*].

Two more [aspects of *Leah*] add to them; one of infancy and one of growth, because of the multiplication of the lights.

Those are the eighteen wives allowed to the king.

ז. ד׳ מוחין דגדלות וד׳ מוחין דקטנות, הרי ח׳. התחילו של גדלות ליכנס, ולא גמרו של קטנות לצאת, הרי ח׳ אחרות. ושתים אחרות נוספות עליהם – א׳ מקטנות וא׳ מגדלות, מפני ריבוים של אורות. אלו י״ח נשים שהמלך מותר בהם.

h) Higher than all the *Partsufim,* is *'Atik,* it is the *Mal'hut* of *Adam Kadmon,* which became *'Atik* in *Atsilut.* Similarly in *Beriah,* for *Mal'hut* of *Atsilut* [621], and in *Yetsirah* [622], and 'Asiah[623].

ח. למעלה מן הפרצופים - עתיק, זו מלכותו של א״ק שנעשית עתיק באצילות. כנגד זה בבריאה - ממלכותה של אצילות ; וכן יצירה, וכן עשיה.

---

[621] Becomes *Atik* in *Beriah*
[622] *Mal'hut* of *Beriah* becomes *Atik* in *Yetsirah*

'Atik is masculine and feminine; masculine in his front, and feminine in his back. The [three] first [*Sephirot*] of *Nukvah* [of *'Atik*] are higher than *Atsilut*, this is the *Radl'a*[624].

The [seven] lower *Sephirot*[625] dress in *Arikh Anpin:*

'Hesed [of 'Atik] in *Keter* [of *Arikh Anpin*],

Gevurah in 'Hokhma,

Tiferet in Binah,

the first parts of *NHY* [of *'Atik*] in *HGT*,

the second [parts of *NHY*] in *NHY*,

the third [parts] of *Netsah* and *Hod*, together with *Mal'hut* [of 'Atik], in *Mal'hut* [of *Arikh Anpin*].

[From there] They come out and illuminate all the other worlds.

עתיק - דכר ונוקבא,

זכר בפניו ונוק׳ באחוריו.

ראשונות של נוק׳ למעלה מאצילות,

זו רדל״א.

תחתונות שבה מתלבשים בא״א :

חסד בכתר,

גבורה בחכמה,

ת״ת בבינה,

פרקים ראשונים של נה״י בחג״ת,

ושניים בנה״י,

ושלישים שבנו״ה ומלכות עמהם - במלכות.

יוצאים ומאירים בכל שאר העולמות.

---

[623] *Mal'hut* of *Yetsirah* becomes *Atik* in *'Asiah*
[624] The Unknown Head
[625] Of *Nukvah* of *Atik*

Eighth chapter

a) [There are] Three heads in *Atika* [626] [*Arikh Anpin*]; *Radl'a* [627], *Gulgolta* and *Mo'ha* [628]. Two that make three [629]: *Gulgolta, Avirah* and *Mo'ha,* the *Da'at* of *'Atik* is hidden in *Avirah.* By these [630], all the worlds are directed with kindness, rigor and mercy.

b) The interiority of the heads [631] : הוי״ה, the exteriority : אהי״ה.
The first ones [632] [are of the aspect] of ע״ב and his אהי״ה,
the seconds [633] [are of the aspect] of ס״ג,
the thirds [634] [are of the aspect] of מ״ה.

פרק שמיני

א. תלת רישין בעתיקא :
רישא דלא אתידע, גלגלתא,
ומוחא.
ב׳ נעשים ג׳ : גלגלתא אוירא
ומוחא ;
דעתו של עתיק גנוז באוירא.
באלו מתנהגים כל העולמות
בחסד בדין וברחמים.

ב. פנימיותן של רישין - הוי״ה,
החצוניות - אהי״ה.
הראשונים דע״ב ואהי״ה שלו,
השניים דס״ג,
השלישיים דמ״ה.

---

[626] In the two *Adarot* of Rabbi Shimon Bar Yohai, *Arich Anpin* is called *Atika*
[627] The unknown head
[628] In the first *Atsilut*
[629] In the second *Atsilut*
[630] The three heads
[631] Is of the aspect of הוי״ה
[632] In the first head ; *Gulgolta - Keter*
[633] In the second head ; *Avirah*

For each [head] there are [three levels of lights]: Interior, encircling [*Makif*], and encircling of the encircling [*Makif* of *Makif*].

פנימי ומקיף ומקיף דמקיף בכל אחת ואחת.

They differentiate by their *Nekudot*[635].
The first letters have the vowels as pronounced – interiority
The *Miluy*[636] has vowels as pronounced – encircling
The *Miluy* has *Kamatz* as a vowel, and the first letters have vowels as pronounced – encircling of encircling. This is the first head. [*Gulgolta*]

במה הם מתפרשים ?
- בניקודיהם.
מנוקד הפשוט בתנועותיו - זה פנימי ;
מנוקד המלוי, כפשוטו - זה המקיף ;
מנוקד המלוי כולו קמץ, והפשוט בתנועותיו –
זה מקיף דמקיף,
זה הראש הראשון.

The first letters have the vowels as pronounced, and *Segol* instead of *Tsere*.
The *Miluy* has vowels as pronounced.
The *Miluy* has *Kamatz* as a vowel. This is the second

מנוקד הפשוט בתנועותיו, מקום צירי סגול ;
מנוקד המלוי כפשוטו.
מנוקד המלוי כולו קמץ –
זה הראש השני.

---

[634] In the third head; *Mo'ha* - *'Hokhma*
[635] Vowels
[636] Letters that are added for the spelling of each individual letter

head. [*Avirah*]

The first letters have the vowels as pronounced, *Segol* instead of *Tsere* and *Patah* instead of *Kamatz*.
The *Miluy* has vowels as pronounced
The *Miluy* has *Patah* as a vowel. This is the third head. [*Mo'ha Stimaah*]

מנוקד הפשוט בתנועותיו,
מקום צירי סגול ומקום קמץ
פתח ;
מנוקד המלוי כפשוטו ;
מנוקד המלוי כולו פתח —
זה הראש השלישי .

c) [There are] Seven *Tikunim* of the head [of *Arikh Anpin*], that are revealed from the seven [lower *Sephirot*] of 'Atik, their indication is:

ג. שבעה תיקוני רישא משבעה של עתיק,
סימנם : ג״ט קר״יע פ״ח.

ג״ט קר״יע פ״ח
From *'Hesed* of *'Atik* - גולגלתא לבנה
(*Gulgolta Levanah*) of Arikh

גולגלתא לבנה . מחסדו של עתיק.

From his *Gevurah* - טלא דבדולחא
(*Tela Debadulha*) of Arikh

טלא דבדולחא מגבורה שלו.

From his *Tiferet* - קרומא דאוירא
(*Kroma Deavirah*) of Arikh

קרומא דאוירא . מת״ת שלו.

רעוא דמצחא - מיסוד שלו.

---

[637] Of *Netsah* and *Hod*

From his *Yesod* - רעוא דמצחא
(*Raava Demitsha*) of *Arikh*

From the first parts of *Netsah* and *Hod* that are higher than *Yesod* - עמר נקי
(*Amer Naki*) of *Arikh*

עמר נקי מראשיתם של נו"ה, שהם גבוהים מן היסוד.

From their last parts[637] – פקיחו דעינין
(*Pekihu Deinin*) of *Arikh*

פקיחו דעיינין מסופם.

From *Mal'hut* – חותמא,
(*Hotmah*)

חוטמא - ממלכות.

Leah and *Ra'hel* – שני נחירים
(*Shene Nehirim*) of *Arikh*

ב' נחירים - לאה ורחל.

d) The [other] *Tikunim* of *Arikh Anpin*:
דיקנא[638], חיורתי[639], נימין[640]
(*Dikna, 'Hivarti, Nimin*)
[There are] Three הוי"ה in each head [of *Arikh Anpin*], and one [641] that contains them.

ד. תיקוניו של א"א :
נימין, חיורתי, ודיקנא.
שלש הויות בכל ראש
ואחת כוללת אותם.

Three הוי"ה, [make a total of] twelve letters, plus the

שלש הויות י"ב אותיות,
ואחת שקוללתן, הרי י"ג.

---

[638] The beard

[639] The white on the scalp between the hair

[640] The extremities of the hairs on the head

[641] One more הוי"ה in each head, which contains the three others

one [642] containing them; make thirteen.

Thirteen חיורתי ('Hivarti), from the three [הוי״ה], in Keter, their place is between the thirteen נימין (Nimin) between each נימא (Nima).	י״ג חיורתי - משלש שבכתר, מקומם בין י״ג נימין, בין נימא לנימא.
Thirteen נימין (Nimin), from the three [הוי״ה], in Avirah.	י״ג נימין משלש שבאוירא.
Thirteen Tikunim of דיקנא (Dikna), from the three [הוי״ה], in 'Hokhma.	י״ג תיקוני דיקנא משלש שבחכמה.
e) [There are] Thirteen Tikunim of דיקנא (Dikna) [of Arikh Anpin]: **אל רחום..** **מי אל כמוך. . נושא עון...**	**ה.** י״ג תיקוני דיקנא : אל רחום וכו׳ ; מי אל כמוך נושא עון וכו׳.
First Tikun: - The two Peot[643]	תיקון א׳ : ב׳ פאות.

---

[642] The extra הוי״ה is counted as one letter only

[643] Hair on each side of the face

Second Tikun:	תיקון ב׳ : שערות שבשפה עליונה.
- The hair on the upper lip	
Third Tikun:	תיקון ג׳ : אורח תחות חוטמא.
- The vacant space under the nose	
Fourth Tikun:	תיקון ד׳ : שבשפה התחתונה.
- The hair on the lower lip	
Fifth Tikun:	תיקון ה׳ : אורח תחות פומא.
- The space under the mouth	תיקון ו׳ : רחבה של זקן.
Sixth Tikun:	
- The width of the beard	תיקון ז׳ : שני תפוחים שנפנו.
Seventh Tikun:	
- The two upper sides of the cheeks	תיקון ח׳ : שטח עליון - מזל נוצר.
Eighth Tikun:	
- [The beard on] The upper chin (*Mazal Notser*)	ט׳ : שערות שבין מזל למזל. תיקון
Ninth Tikun:	
- The hair between the upper and lower chin	תיקון י׳ : שערות הגרון .
Tenth Tikun:	
- The hair on the throat	תיקון י״א : שכולם שוין.
Eleventh Tikun:	
- They are all equal	תיקון י״ב : פה פנוי.
Twelfth Tikun:	
- The free mouth	תיקון י״ג : שטח תחתון – מזל ונקה.
Thirteen Tikun:	
- [The beard under] The	

---

[644] Where there is the head of *Z'A*

lower chin (*Mazal Nake*)
The length of the *Mazalot* is
until the navel[644].

שיעורם של מזלות עד הטבור.

f) The *Tikunim* of Z'A:
מ''צל .
צ – interior *Mo'hin*,
ל, מ – encircling *Mo'hin*.
When they came out, they
were four [645] ; this
corresponds to the מ.
[They became] Three [646]
when they returned in the
Keli of *Imah;* this
corresponds to the ל, and
nine [647] [*Mo'hin*] were
realized inside of him; this
corresponds to the צ.

The four [648] ; are from
KHBD of *Imah*[649], the three
are from HGT[650], and the
nine are from NHY[651].

ו. תיקוניו של ז''א : צל''ם.

צ' . מוחין פנימים,

ל' מ' - מקיפין שבו.

שבשעה שיצאו היו ד', זה מ' שלו.

חזרו שלשה בכליה של אי', זה ל'.

וט' נעשו בגופו, זה צ'.

של ד' בכחב''ד דאימא,

של ג' בחג''ת,

של ט' בנה''י.

---

[645] '*Hokhma* and *Binah*, '*Hasadim* and *Gevurot*
[646] '*Hokhma* and *Binah*, '*Hasadim* and *Gevurot* became one
[647] The *NHY* of *Tevunah* spread in him in nine aspects
[648] The first four *Mo'hin*
[649] This will make his second encircling *Mo'hin*
[650] This will make his encircling *Mo'hin*
[651] This will make his interior *Mo'hin*

g) From *Z'A* there are: נימין [652], חיורתי [653], דיקנא [654] (*Nimin, 'Hivarti, Dikna*) From *Arikh Anpin*, they are thirteen [*Tikunim*]. From *Z'A* they are nine [*Tikunim*]. When his *Tikun* [of *Z'A*] is complete, they become thirteen.

ז. נימין חיורתי ודיקנא בז״א.

של א״א - י״ג,

של ז״א - ט׳.

כשנשלם תיקונו נשלמים לי״ג.

h) From the forehead of *Z'A*, emerge and spurt out from the four *Mo'hin*[655]; the four parashiot of the *Tefilin*. Their garments are their compartments.

ח. במצחו של ז״א

בוקעים ויוצאים מד׳ מוחין

ד׳ פרשיות של תפילין,

ומלבושיהם - בתים שלהם.

They are ten *Sephirot*[656]: *HBD* are the *Tefilin*[657], *'Hesed* and *Gevurah* are the straps of the head, *Tiferet* is the knot on the back; it is from there, that

עשר ספירות הם :

חב״ד בתפילין .

חו״ג ברצועות של הראש .

ת״ת בקשר מלאחריהם,

שמשם יוצאת לאה ;

ב׳ רצועות יורדות - נו״ה,

נצח עד החזה, והוד עד הטבור.

---

[652] The extremities of the hairs on the head

[653] The white on the scalp between the hair

[654] The beard

[655] *'Hokhma, Binah,* and *Daat* which is divided in two; *'Hasadim* and *Gevurot*

[656] From the encircling *Mo'hin* – The *Tefilin* of the head

[657] Of the head

Leah comes out.

The two straps that come down are *Netsah* and *Hod*; *Netsah* until the chest, and *Hod* until the navel.

In the *Tefilin* from *Imah*:

קדש, והיה כי יביאך, שמע, והיה אם שמוע

In the *Tefilin* from *Abah*:

קדש, והיה כי יביאך, והיה אם שמוע, שמע

i) A light from *Imah* encircles *Z'A*; this is the white *Talit*.

The hair of *Z'A* appears after his growth ministered by *Imah*; when her new *NHY*[658] are extending on his rear [659] and reach his thorax [660]. They [the lights [661]] are encircling around *Z'A*, and encircling on the head of *Nukvah*.

Encircling of *Z'A* – his *Talit*

Encircling of *Nukvah* – his *Tsitsit*.

תפילין מאימא:

קדש, והיה כי יביאך, שמע, והיה אם שמוע.

תפילין מאבא:

קדש, והיה כי יביאך, והיה אם שמוע, שמע.

ט. ואור מאימא מקיפו לז"א, זהו טלית לבנה - שערות של ז"א, אחר גדלותו ששרתה עליו אימא, והגיעו נה"י שלה חדשים מאחוריו עד החזה, מקיף לז"א ומקיף על ראש נוקבא.

מקיפו של ז"א - טלית, מקיפה של נוקבא - ציצית שבו.

---

[658] Of *Imah*

[659] Of *Z'A*

[660] Of *Z'A*

[661] His hair

j) The *Tikunim* of *Nukvah*[662] are:

Fifteen נימין (*Nimin*) on her head [663] ; their color is purple.

Six *Tikunim* on her face, from the six *Tikunim* of the *Dikna* [of *Z'A*]. When they are complete, they are nine [*Tikunim*].

k) Her *Tefilin* [of the head of *Ra'hel*] are on the hand of *Z'A*, they bind on his left, as it is said:

"Set me as a seal upon your heart, as a seal upon your arm" (Shir Hashirim, 8, 6)

They [the *Mo'hin* of *Nukvah*] are built by *Netsah* and *Hod* of *Z'A*. In them,[664] are *'Hokhma* and *Binah* of *Imah,* and *'Hokhma* and

 י. תיקוניה של נוק' –
ט״ו נימין בראשה, וצבעם ארגמ״ין.
וששה תיקונים בפניה מששה
תיקוני דיקנא.
כשהם נשלמים נעשים ט'.

יא. תפילין שלה - של יד לז״א,
שהם נקשרים בשמאל שלו,
שנאמר (שיר השירים ח, ו) :
"שימני כחותם על לבך כחותם
על זרועך".

ומנו״יה דז״א הם נעשים,
שבהם חו״ב מאימא וחו״ב מאבא.

---

662 *Ra'hel*
663 From there, the hair comes out
664 *Netsah* and *Hod*

Binah of *Abah*[665].

The ones of *Abah* make her [*Mo'hin* of] *'Hokhma* and *Binah*.	של אבא נעשים לה לחו״ב,
The ones of *Imah* make her [*Mo'hin* of] *'Hasadim* and *Gevurot*, they[666] end in one single compartment [667], because *Netsah* and *Hod* make two parts of one single body.	ושל אימא נעשים לה לחו״ג, נכללים בבית אחד, שנו״ה פלגי גופא
l) *Yesod* of *Abah* is preponderant between his own *Netsah* and *Hod*; he stands in *Yesod* of *Imah*, and is preponderant between her *Netsah* and *Hod*. Therefore, there are four lights in him[668], and from them emerge the *Tefilin* on the forehead of *Ya'acov*[669].	**יב.** יסוד אבא מכריע בין נו״ה שלו, עומד ביסוד אימא ומכריע בין נו״ה שלה ; נמצאו בו ד׳ אורות שמהם תפילין במצחו של יעקב.

---

[665] *Abah* and *Imah* make the *Mo'hin* of *'Hokhma* in *Netsah* of *Z'A*, and the *Mo'hin* of *Binah* in *Hod* of *Z'A*

[666] The four *Parashiot*

[667] The *Tefilin* of the hand

[668] *Yesod* of *Abah*

[669] *Tefilin* on the arm of *Rabenu Tam*

These[670] and these[671] come out from Ya'acov, and make the Tefilin on his forehead. They[672] return to the back, and tie a knot behind him. They[673] return, and emerge [through Ya'acov], and then by the forehead of Ra'hel to make the Tefilin on her head[674].

The ones [675] of Yesod of Abah remain in Ya'acov, the ones of Netsah and Hod of Z'A remain for Ra'hel; they[676] return to the back, and tie a knot behind her [Ra'hel].
[The order of the Parashiot] Of Ra'hel: קדש, והיה כי יביאך, שמע, והיה אם שמוע
[The order of the Parashiot] Of Ya'acov: the two והיה, follow.

אלו ואלו יוצאים ביעקב ונעשים תפילין במצחו.
חוזרים לאחוריהם וקושרים קשר מאחריו.
חוזרים ויוצאים,
עד שיוצאים במצחה של רחל,
נעשים תפילין בראשה.

של יסוד אבא נשארים ביעקב.
של נו"ה דז"א נשארים לרחל.
חוזרים לאחור וקושרים קשר באחוריה.
של רחל : קדש, והיה כי יביאך, שמע, והיה אם שמוע.
של יעקב : הויות להדדי.

---

[670] The four lights in Yesod of Abah
[671] The lights of Netsah and Hod of Z'A
[672] The lights in Yesod of Abah – Or Hozer (returning lights)
[673] The lights of Netsah and Hod of Z'A - Or Hozer (returning lights)
[674] Of Ra'hel
[675] Lights
[676] The lights of Netsah and Hod of Z'A
[677] From the Yud

The *Yesod* of *Z'A* is between the shoulders of *Ra'hel;* this is the י *(Yud)* [knot] of the (arm's) *Tefilin.* A strap comes out from it[677], to build the *Nukvah.*

Three wrappings on the biceps; corresponding to the three first (*Sephirot*) [*G'aR* of *Nukvah*]

Seven on the forearm; corresponding to the seven lower (*Sephirot*) [*Z'aT* of *Nukvah*]

Three on the finger; corresponding to the *NHY* [of *Z'A*] in her *Mo'hin.*

m) A world comprise *Adam* [*Partsuf*], his garment, his encircling, and his *Hechalot.*

Adam[678] how? This is the *Tikun* [the structure] of the

יסודו של ז״א בין כתפיה של רחל,
זה יו״ד שבתפילין.
ורצועה יוצאה ממנה לבנינה של
נוק׳.

ג׳ כריכות בקיבורת - ג״ר,
ז׳ בזרוע : ז״ת,
ג׳ באצבע . נה״י שבמוחיה.

יג. כללו של עולם :
אדם, ולבושו, מקיפיו, והיכלו.

אדם כיצד ?
זה תיקונו של פרצופו .

---

[678] The *Partsuf* is named *Adam* (man). Like the body of man, which has 613 members, a *Partsuf* has 613 lights

[679] *Sephira* or *Partsuf*

[680] Of the *Sephira* or *Partsuf*

Partsuf – 248 limbs and 365 veins, *NRN* within him, and *'Hayah* and *Ye'hidah* encircling on him.

רמ״ח איברים ושס״ה גידים. נר״ן בתוכו, ח״י מקיפים עליו.

The light descended to enter in him [679]; a part entered, and a part remained outside; because the *Keli*[680] was not able to contain it. It encircled his *Keli,* and encircled what was under it [681] . [Linear encircling lights]

ירד האור ליכנס בתוכו, חלק נכנס, וחלק נשאר בחוץ, שאין הכלי יכול להגבילו, מקיף לכליו, ומקיף לכל מה שתחתיו.

From what entered [of the lights], it [682] returned upward, came out, and only encircled its own *Keli*[683] . [Returning encircling lights]

וממה שנכנס - חוזר ויוצא לחוץ ומקיף על כליו בלבד.

There are then two types of encircling lights:
Linear [of the aspect of *Ye'hidah*], and returning [of the aspect of *'Hayah*].

אלו שני מקיפים : ישר וחוזר.

---

[681] The lower *Sephirot*
[682] Some parts of lights
[683] Of the *Sephira*

n) His *Levush* how [is it realized]? From the striking [of the interior lights of the *Partsuf*] against each other, a *Levush* was made, which covers them [684] on the outside[685].

יד. לבושו כיצד ?
מהכאותיהם של אורות נעשה
לבוש עליהם מבחוץ.

There is *Hashma'T*[686] from *Imah* for *Z'uN*, when her *NHY*[687] entered in him [*Z'A*], her skin, flesh, bones and veins[688] included with his[689]. With the exception of [some of] her skin[690] that remained in surplus outside, and covers him because of the eyes of the exteriority[691].

וחשמ"ל יש לזו"ן מאימא,
שבשעה שנכנסו נה"י שלה בתוכו –
עור ובשר ועצמות וגידין נכללו
שלה בשלו,
חוץ מן העור שנמצא עודף על שלו
מבחוץ,
ומכסה עליו מפני עיניהם של
חיצונים .

o) The *Hechalot* are to a *Partsuf,* as a house is to a man. The Malhuts[692] of the *Sephirot* [are] their

טו. היכלות לפרצוף כבתים
לאדם.
מלכויותיהם של ספירות -
חיצוניות שלהם,

---

[684] For each *Partsuf*
[685] Of the *Partsuf*
[686] Name of the *Levush*
[687] Of *Imah*
[688] Of *Imah*
[689] Skin, flesh, bones and veins
[690] Of *Imah*
[691] The external force – *Sitra A'hra*
[692] The *Mal'hut* of each *Sephira*

exteriority [693] ; [they are] their *Hechalot*. The image of man [the nine superior *Sephirot*], is their interiority.

אלו ההיכלות.
ודמות אדם – פנימיות בתוכם.

These are not the only types [of aspects] of interiority and exteriority; there are others[694]. However, this is the structure in each world; the lights subdivide among themselves [in interiority and exteriority aspects].

לא שאין פנימיות וחיצוניות אלא זה,
אלא שזהו חילוקו של עולם .
חוזרים ומתחלקים כל אחד בשלו.

p) There are seven *Hechalot*: [in *Beriah*]
First - לבנת הספיר (*Livnat Hasapir*)
Second - עצם השמים (*Etsem Hashamayim*)
Third – נוגה (*Nogah*)
Fourth – זכות (*Zehut*)
Fifth – אהבה

טז. ז' היכלות הם :

לבנת הספיר,

עצם השמים,

נוגה,

זכות,

אהבה,

---

[693] Of the *Sephirot* or the *Partsufim*

[694] It is not only the *Malhuts* that are exteriorities; there are many other aspects that also divide in interiority and exteriority

[695] Glory of (*Kiseh Hakavod*) Throne of glory - *Mal'hut* of *Atsilut*

[696] *Kodesh Kodashim* - (קדש קדשים)

(Ahavah)

Sixth – רצון

(Ratson)

רצון,

Seventh - קדש קדשים

(Kodesh Kodashim)

ק״ק.

[Corresponding to:]

First *Hechal*

- *Yesod* and *Mal'hut*

היכל יסוד ומלכות : אחד.

.

Second *Hechal*

- *Hod*

היכל הוד - אחד

Third *Hechal*

- *Netsah*

היכל נצח - אחד.

Fourth *Hechal*

- *Gevurah*

היכל גבורה - אחד.

Fifth *Hechal*

- *'Hesed*

היכל חסד - אחד.

Sixth *Hechal*

- *Tiferet*

היכל ת״ת - אחד.

Seventh *Hechal*

- The three first [*Sephirot*]

היכל ג׳ ראשונות - אחד.

These are the seven *Hechalot* in *Beriah*, in them; the *Kav*od [glory] of the *Makom*[695] spreads out. Each [*Hechal*] has *Nefesh* and *Rua'h,* and the *Kav*od is their *Neshama* in the seventh *Hechal*[696].

אלו ז׳ היכלות שבבריאה,
שבהם כבודו של מקום מתפשט
בתוכם.
נפש ורוח לכל אחד,
והכבוד נשמה להם בהיכל השביעי.

There are three functions

וג׳ דברים משמשים :

[for the *Hechalot*]:
- Separate beings attach to their root.
- The *Tsadikim* enjoy the presence of the *Shekhina*.
- The angels receive from [through] them their tasks.

נקשרים בהם התחתונים בשרשם,
ונהנים הצדיקים מזיו השכינה,
ומלאכי השרת מקבלים מהם
פעולתם.

q) At the end[697] of *Atsilut*, there is a curtain; it is made from the lights of *Imah*.

יז. בסופו של אצילות - מסך,
מאורה של אימא הוא נעשה.

[From this curtain] *Hashma'l* comes down and encircles *Z'uN* underneath its legs. The lights of *Atsilut* pass through it[698], and make *Beriah*. Thus, *Beriah* is of the [aspect] secret of *Imah*.

חשמ״ל יורד ומקיף מתחת רגליהם
של זו״ן,
ואורות של אצילות עוברים בו
ועושים בריאה.
נמצאה בריאה מסודה של אימא.

From it [*Beriah*] to *Yetsirah*, there are two curtains: A curtain from *Imah* to *Z'uN*, and a curtain from *Z'A* to *Nukvah*. Thus, *Yetsirah* is from the [aspect] secret of *Z'A*.

ממנה ליצירה מסך על מסך:
מסך מאימא לזו״ן, ומסך מז״א
לנוק׳.
נמצאת יצירה מסודו של ז״א.

From it [*Yetsirah*] to *'Asiah*,

ממנה לעשייה מסך על שנים:

---

[697] At the bottom
[698] Curtain

one curtain on two [curtains]: One curtain from *Imah* to *Z'uN*, one curtain from *Z'A* to *Nukvah*, and one curtain from *Nukvah* to the world under her. Thus, *'Asiah* is of from the [aspect] secret of *Nukvah*.

מסך מאי׳ לזו״ן, ומסך מז״א לנוקבא,
מסך מנוק׳ לעולם שתחתיה .
נמצאת עשייה מסודה של נוק ׳ .

r) The name of *Atsilut* is[699] *'AV*.

יח. שמו של אצילות - ע״ב.

SaG, *MaH* and *BaN* descended [700] to *Beriah*, *Yetsirah* and *'Asiah*. They returned and ascended: *MaH* ascended and clothed *SaG*, *BaN* ascended and clothed *MaH*.

ירדו ס״ג מ״ה ב״ן לבי״יע.
חזרו ועלו.
עלה מ״ה והלביש על ס״ג,
עלה ב״ן והלביש על מ״ה.

Thus, *BaN* is on top of all, this is the *Mahakey* [701] [מעקה]; [a fence] for the endings of the lights not to be uncovered when they are below, so that the *Klipot*[702] will not attach to them. As

נמצא ב״ן למעלה מכולן, זה מעקה,
שלא יהיה סיומם של אורות כשהם למטה,
ולא יהיו הקליפות אוחזות בהם,
שנאמר (דברים כב, ח) :
"ועשית מעקה לגגך

---

[699] From the aspect of the name of *'AV* – miluy of 72
[700] When the *Kelim* broke
[701] Parapet or railing
[702] Husks (negative forces)

it is said:

"You shall make a parapet for your roof, that you should not bring any blood upon your house, if any man falls from there" (Devarim, 22, 8)

ולא תשים דמים בביתך כי יפול הנופל ממנו".

s) These are the four worlds on which the Lord solely reigns, on all his work. The service of the creatures is in all of them [703]. The uniqueness [**יקוק**] of the *Ein Sof B'H*, is sovereign over all[704]. Like the master of the prophets said:

"Hear Israel H' is our G-d H' is One" (Devarim, 10, 4)

יט. אלו ד' עולמות שבהם מולך אדון יחיד על מעשיו. עבודתם של תחתונים בכולם. ויחודו של א"ס ב"ה מתיחד בכולם. הוא שרבן של נביאים אומר (דברים י, ד): "שמע ישראל ה' אלהינו ה' אחד".

---

[703] To make the *Tikun* of all the worlds
[704] The four worlds

Ninth chapter

a) From the *Sephirot,* there are three ramifications: the angels, the *Sitra A'hra*, and *Neshamot* (physical entities). For each mission, there is one angel. The *Sephirot* decree; the angels accomplish. As it is said: "Bless the Lord, O you his angels, you mighty ones, who do His word, listening to the voice of His word" (Tehilim, 103, 20)

b) The *Sitra A'hra,* how [is it built]? As it is said: "I form the light, and create darkness; I make peace, and create evil". (Isaiah, 45, 7) He forms the light; this is the right, He creates the obscurity; this is the left, He makes peace; these are the angels of peace, and creates evil; this is S'M[705].

The angels of peace make

א. תולדותיהם של ספירות ג' : מלאכים, סטרא אחרא (גשמים) [ונשמות].

לכל שליחות - מלאך.

הספירות גוזרות והמלאך עושה, שנאמר (תהלים קג, כ) :

"ברכו ה' מלאכיו גבורי כח עושי דברו לשמוע בקול דברו".

ב. ס״א כיצד -

זהו שנאמר (ישעיה מה, ז) :

"יוצר אור ובורא חושך עושה שלום ובורא רע".

יוצר אור - זה הימין,

ובורא חושך - זהו בשמאל,

עושה שלום - אלו מלאכי שלום,

ובורא רע - זה סמ'

מלאכי שלום - עשר כתות,

---

[705] Initials of the main negative angel
[706] The lower side, (opposite side)

ten groups; they serve the ten *Sephirot* of the right.

The angels of destruction make ten levels; they serve the ten *Sephirot* from the left side[706]. About them, he says:

"G-d also made this one, facing the other" (Kohelet, 7, 14)

משמשין לעשר ספירות של ימין.
מלאכי חבלה - עשר מדריגות,
משמשין לעשר ספירות מצד שמאל.
עליהם הוא אומר (קהלת ז, יד):
"גם את זה לעומת זה עשה האלהים".

c) Four levels - four *Klipot* (husks), these are the worlds of *S'M*. They obstruct the lights of the *Sephirot*, and conceal him[707]. Because of the [bad] deeds of the lower beings,[708] they[709] come and do evil in the world.

ג. ד' מדריגות - ד' קליפות,
עולמיו של סמ',
סותמים אורם של ספירות
ומסלקים אותו,
במעשה התחתונים באים,
ועושים רעה בעולם:

[There are four *Klipot*]:
- נגה - (*Nogah*) -
- Glow
- ענן דול - (Anan Gadol) -
- A large cloud
- אש מתלקחת - (Eish

נוגה,

ענן גדול,

ואש מתלקחת,

---

[707] They conceal man from his root, and from the light
[708] Man
[709] The destructive angels

Mitlakahat)
- A dividing fire
- רוח סערה (*Rua'h* Sehara)
- A wind of storm.

ורוח סערה ;

As it is written in Ezekhiel:
"And I looked, and behold, a stormy wind came from the north, a great cloud, a fire flaring up, and a glow was around it, and out of its midst; like the *Hashma'l*" (Ezekiel, 1, 4)

שכן מפורשים ע"י יחזקאל (א, ד) :
"וארא והנה רוח סערה באה
מן־הצפון ענן גדול
ואש מתלקחת ונגה לו סביב
ומתוכה כעין החשמל מתך האש"

d) Four *Klipot* - four worlds for each. In them [each world]; there are five *Partsufim* in ten *Sephirot*.

ד. ד' קליפות - ד' עולמות לכל אחת,
שבם ה' פרצופים בעשר ספירות,

The *Tikunim* of the lower beings are in the four [superior] worlds [of ABYA], and the deterioration [they cause] reach the four [lower] worlds. If the lower beings merit, the Lord guides with mercy, and the "policeman" disregards. If they sin, the Merciful departs, and the "policeman" acts with rigor on the guilty. It is only

שתיקוניהם של תחתונים בד' עולמות,
ופגמיהם בד' עולמות.
זכו התחתונים -
האדון מנהג ברחמים, והשוטר עובר מפניו.
חטאו -
בעל הרחמים נסתלק, והשוטר עושה דין בחייבים.
בסילוקו של אדון מעשהו של שוטר,
הוא שנאמר (במדבר יב, ט-י) :
"ויחר אף ה' בם וילך והענן סר

when the Lord departs, that the "policeman" acts. As it is said:

"The anger of the Lord was kindled against them, and He departed, the cloud left the tent, and behold, Miriam had become leprous, white as snow." (Bamidbar, 12, 9, 10)

e) The roots of the *Klipot*[710] proceed from the order of the rigors[711]. By them[712], she is subdued, and by them, she is amplified depending on the deeds of the lower beings. As it is written:

"You shall therefore keep My statutes, and My judgments; which if a man does, he shall live in them" (Vayikra, 18, 5)

מעל האהל
והנה מרים מצורעת כשלג".

ה. סדרי הדינים -
אלה שרשים של קליפות,
מהם מכניעים אותה, ומהם -
מגביהים אותה,
לפי מעשיהם של תחתונים.
הוא שהכתוב אומר (ויקרא יח, ה) :

"ושמרתם את חוקותי ואת משפטי
אשר יעשה אותם האדם וחי
בהם".

---

[710] This root is from the side of the *Kedusha*

[711] The rears of the *Sephirot*

[712] The rears of the *Sephirot*

Tenth chapter

a) The service to the Lord is done by the souls. It has five names: *Nefesh, Rua'h, Neshama, 'Hayah* and *Ye'hidah*, [their roots are] from the five *Partsufim*. *'Hayah* and *Ye'hidah* are from *Atsilut, Neshama* from *Beriah, Rua'h* from *Yetsirah,* and *Nefesh* from *'Asiah.*

Therefore, the force of man is from *Mal'hut* of *'Asiah,* until *Keter* of *Atsilut*. As it is said:
"Let Us make man in Our image, after Our likeness; and let them have dominion over the creatures of the sea." (Bereshit, 1, 26)

b) The *Tikun* of the soul is realized by the *Gilgul* [reincarnation], and the *Ibur* [attachment].

How? The service of the soul is the accomplishment of the 613 *Mitsvot*, if it

פרק עשירי

א. עבודתו של מקום - לנשמות.
ה׳ שמות הם : נר״נ ח״י, מה׳
פרצופים.
חיה יחידה מאצילות,
נשמה מבריאה,
רוח מיצירה,
נפש מעשייה.

נמצא כחו של אדם
ממלכותו של עשייה עד כתרו של
אצילות.
זהו שנאמר (בראשית א, כו) :
"נעשה אדם בצלמנו כדמותנו
וירדו בדגת הים".

ב. תיקוניה של נשמה - גלגול
ועיבור.

כיצד ?
עבודתה של נשמה תרי״ג מצוות,
השלימתם - עולה למנוחה,

accomplishes them; it ascends to rest, if not; it comes back and reincarnates. It does not reincarnate completely, only its parts that need the *Tikun* do.

ואם לאו - חוזרת ומתגלגלת.
לא כולה מתגלגלת,
אלא חלקיה הצריכים תיקון .

c) What is a *Gilgul*, and what is an *Ibur*: The *Gilgul* is [the reincarnation of a soul] from the time of birth until death, the *Ibur* [is an attachment of another soul to his, which] could come and leave anytime.

ג. איזהו גלגול ואיזהו עיבור ?
גלגול - משעת לידה ועד מיתה ;
עיבור - ביאתו בכל שעה, ויציאתו
בכל שעה.

For the *Mitsvot* that it was obligated to accomplish, it accomplishes them by the *Gilgul*, for the ones it did not have to accomplish;[713] it accomplishes them by the *Ibur;* which departs afterwards.

מצוות שנתחייבה בהם -
משלימתם בגלגול,
ושלא נתחייבה בהם - בעיבור
משלימתם, והולכת לה.

The *Tsadikim* reincarnate up to a thousand generations, the sinners, up

צדיקים מתגלגלים לאלפים,
רשעים עד רבעים,
שנא' (עמוס א, ג) :

---

[713] *Mitsvot* that were not possible for him to accomplish as: Circumcision for a son he did not have etc.

to four. As it is said
"But for the fourth I will
not turn away." (Amos, 1,3)

"ועל ארבעה לא אשיבנו".

d) *Nefesh* comes first, after
it comes *Rua'h*, after it
Neshama, and after them
come *'Hayah* and *Ye'hidah*.
There are garments
[envelopes] for each soul.
Nefesh, *Rua'h* and *Neshama*
reincarnate independently.

ד. נפש בא בתחלה,
ואחריו רוח,
ואחריו נשמה,
וח"י אחריהן.
לכל נשמה לבושים.
מתגלגלת נפש לבדה ורוח לבדו
ונשמה לבדה.

Souls could mount on
garments [envelopes] not of
their sort. Not all the souls
are equal, the new are not
like the old, and the
reincarnated once is not like
the reincarnated twice. On
all [these souls], it is
written:
"And it is turned around by
His guidance, so that they
may do whatever He
commands them ..." (Job,
37, 12)

ומרכיבים נשמות בלבושים שלא
במינם.
לא כל הנשמות שוות :
שלא כחדשות הישנות,
ולא כמגולגלות אחת המגולגלות
שתים.
ועל כולם הוא אומר (איוב לז, יב) :

"והוא מסבות מתהפך
בתחבולותיו לפעלם".

"But devises means, that
none of us be banished".
(Samuel 2, 14, 14)

ואומר (שמואל ב יד, יד) :
"וחשב מחשבות לבלתי ידח
ממנו נדח".

"Every one who is called by My Name; for I have created him for My glory, I have formed him; yes, I have made him".
(Isaiah, 43, 7)

ואומר (ישעיה מג, ז) :
"כל הנקרא בשמי ולכבודי בראתיו יצרתיו אף עשיתיו".

"G-od will reign forever".
(Shemot, 16, 18)

ואומר (שמות טו, יח) :
"ה' ימלוך לעולם ועד".

"And your people shall all be *Tsadikim*; and possess this land forever, a branch of My planting, a work of My hands; for My proudness"

ואומר (ישעיה ס, כא) :
"ועמך כולם צדיקים לעולם ירשו ארץ
נצר מטעי מעשי ידי להתפאר".

Bibliography

In Hebrew

From the Ramhal

כללות האילן הקדוש

פתחי חכמה ודעת

קלח פתחי חכמה

כללים ראשונים

אדיר במרום

From the Ari Z'al

כתבי הארי

עץ חיים

שער רוח הקודש

שער הגלגולים

The Zohar (Rabbi Shimon Bar Yohai)   ספר הזהר

דרך חכמת האמת לרמחל
Rav Mordekhai Chriqui (Editions Ramhal, Jerusalem)

Rav Shalom Oulman (Jerusalem)   האילן הקדוש לרמחל

In French

Rabbi Moshe Hayim Luzzatto, "Le flambeau de la Cabale"
Rav Mordekhai Chriqui (Editions Ramhal, Jerusalem)

The published works of the Ramhal

1) Kalah Pith'e Hokhma
   Koretz,1785, Krakaü,1830, Etc... Jerusalem 1987

2) Pithe Hokhma Vadaat
   Varsovie, 1884, Jerusalem 1961, Bne-Brak 1986

3) Hoker Oumekubal
   Sklov,1784, Lemberg, 1800, Etc.. Bne-Brak 1986

4) Adir Bamarom
   Varsovie,1886, Jerusalem 1961, Jerusalem 1988.

5) Da'at Tevunot
   Varsovie, 1889 and 1891, Bne Brak 1983.

6) Kineat Hachem Tsevaot
   Konigsberg,1862, Bne Brak, 1984

7) Meguilat Setarim
   Varsovie 1889, Jerusalem 1961, Bne Brak 1986.

8) Milhemet Moche

9) Messilat Yecharim
   Published by the author in Amsterdam in 1740.
   Zolkiew,1766, Montoue 1781, Shlov 1784 Etc...
   Jerusalem 1978.

10) Sepher Hakelalim (Richonim)
   Varsovie 1889, Etc... Jerusalem 1961, Bne Brak 1983.

11) Kelalim Cheniyim
   Same Edition, Bne Brak, 1986

12) Kelalut Hailan Hakadoch
   Same Edition, Bne Brak, 1986

13) Binyane 'Olam
   Same Edition

14) Sod Hachem Lireav
   Same Edition

15) Michkenei Elyone
   Bne Brak 1984.

16) Maamar Vayhi Mikets.
   Same Edition

17) Biurim Al Otsroth Hayim
   Same Edition

18) Assara Oroth
   Same Edition

19) Pinot Hamerkava
   Same Edition
20) Tikunim Hahadachim
   Tel Aviv 1958.

21) Kitsur Chaar Hakavanot
   Bne Brak 1978.

22) Massekhet Roch Hachana
     Bne Brak 1978.

23) Taktu Tefilot
     Israël1979.

24) Derekh Hachem
     Amsterdam 1896, Jerusalem 1981.

25) Derekh Tevunot
     Amsterdam 1742, Lemberg 1833, Minsk 1835, Jerusalem
1976.

26) Derekh Kokhma
     Amsterdam 1783, 1785, 1788, Lodz 1913 –

27) Derekh Ets Hayim
     Same Edition

281, 29), 30), 3d Maamar Al Hahagadot, Maamar Haikarim,
Maamar Hahochma, Maamar Hagueoula
Amsterdam 1783, Jerusalem 1965,

32) Sepher Hahigayon
     Varsovie 1897.

33) Lechon Limudim
     Mantoue 1724, Berlin 1750, Israël 1945.

34) Iguereth Hamelitsa
     Novodvor 1796.

35) Maamar Al Hadracha
   Prague 1841.

36) Maasse Chimchone
   Tel *A'viv* 1927.

37) Migdal Oz
   Leipzig, 1837, Lemberg 1850, Tel Aviv 1927, Jerusalem
1972

38) Layecharim Tehila
   Amsterdam 1743, Berlin 1780, Jerusalem 1981.

39) Yam Veyabacha
   Oxford 1853, Londres 1854, Lemberg 1879.

40) Songs and poems
   Venise N.D., Frienze 1910, Frankfort 1910, Paris 1899,
   Vilna 1844,   Krakaü 1892.

41) Shir Hanoukat Haarone
   Venise 1729, Leipzig 1837, Jerusalem 1982.

42), 43), 44)
Maamar Arimat Yadi Betseloutine,
Maamar Hareutine, Maamar Parachat Michpatim
Bne Brak, 1984.

45), 46), 47),48)
Halom Daniel, Richa Vesifa, Heth Adam Harichon,

Arimat Yadi, Chivea Malkin
Jerusalem 1988.

49) Kaf Dalet Kichute Kala
     Jerusalem 1984 ,Varsovie 1889.

Many other writings are not yet published, or have not been
found to this day.

Translated books of the Ramhal

In English

Messilat Yesharim;
The Path of the Just.
Translated by Shraga Silverstein
Publisher: Philipp Feildheim

Da'at Tevunot
The Knowing Heart
Translated by Shraga Silverstein
Publisher: Philipp Feildheim

Derech Hachem
The way of G-d
Translated by: Rav Ariyeh Kaplan
Publisher: Philipp Feildheim

Sepher Haigayon
The book of Logic
Translated by: Rav Chaim Tscholkowsky
Publisher: Philipp Feildheim

Derech Tevunot
The Ways of Reason
Translated by: Rav Chaim Tscholkowsky
Publisher: Philipp Feildheim

Derech Chochmah
The Path of Wisdom
Translated by: Rav Yitzchok Spring

Publisher: Shaarei Chochmah Institute Emanuel

In French

Derekh Hachem
La Voie de D.

Messilat Yesharim
La Voie des Justes

Da'at Tevounot
Les Voies de la Direction Divine

Translated by : Rav Mordekhai Chriqui
Publisher : Editions Ramhal, Jerusalem

Shivhim *Tikunim*
Les Soixante Dix Arrangements 1 and 2
Translated by : Rav. Daniel Cohen
Publisher: Editions Ramhal, Jerusalem

Hoker Oumekoubal
Le Philosophe et le Cabaliste
Translated by: Joëlle Hansel
Publisher : Editions Verdier

Glossary

A"A	Partsuf Arich Anpin
Abah	Partsuf
Abah ve Imah	Father and Mother
Adam Kadmon	Primordial man. World on top of Atsilut
A"K	Adam Kadmon
'Akudim	Bound - Tied (see Olan Ha'Akudim)
Alphin	Plural of the letter Aleph
'Anaf	Branch
'Anafe A"K	Branches of A"K
'Anafim	Branches
Ari Z'al	Rabbi Isaac Louria Ashkenazi. Author of the "Etz Hayim"
Arikh Anpin	Partsuf – Long countenance
Asiah	World of action – of man
ASMB	AV, SaG, MaH, BaN
'Atik	Ancient
'Atik Yomin	Partsuf
'Atika	Ancient
Atsilut	World of emanation
Autiot	Letters
'A"V	Miluy (spelling) of the name YKVK having a total 72
BaN	Miluy (spelling) of the name YKVK with a total of 52
Beriah	World of creation – of the souls
B'H	Barouch Hou (Blessed is He)

Binah	Sephira (understanding)
Boreh	The Creator
Da'at	Sephirah
Dikna	Beard (illuminations of the face)
D"uN	Masculine and feminine
Dvekut	Adhesion - Adherence
E"S	Ein Sof, The without end or limit
Ein Sof	The without end or limit
Elokim	G-d
'Et Ratson	Moment of bounty
'Etz	Tree
'Etz 'Hayim	Tree of life - Master work of the Ari Z'al
Gadlut	Adulthood - Growth
G"aR	The three first Sephirot
Gematria	Numerical values of the letters
Gevul	Boundary - Limit
Gevurah	Sephira - Rigor
Gevurot	Rigors
Gilgul	Reincarnation
Giluy	Revelation - Clarity
Giluy Yi'hudo	Revelation of his unity
Gulgolta	Skull
'Hallal	Space - Vacuum
'Hashmal	Name of a Levush
'Hasadim	Plural of Hesed
'Hayah	Fourth level of the soul

HBD	Hochma, Binah and Daat
Hekhal	Portal - level - Malhut of a Sephira
Hekhalot	Plural of Hekhal
'Hesed	Sephira - Bounty
HGT	Hesed, Gevurah and Tiferet
'Hivarti	The white on the scalp
Hod	Sephira (Glory)
'Hokhma	Parstuf (wisdom)
'Hotem	Nose
'Hozer	Returning
Ibur	Attachment - Gestation
'Igul	Circle
'Igulim	Circular Sephirot
Ilan	Tree
Imah	Partsuf Imah
ISOT	Partsufim Israel Saba and Tevunah
ISOT 2	Second Partsufim of Israel Saba and Tevunah
Israel	Partsuf
Israel Sabbah 1	Partsuf
Israel Sabbah 2	Partsuf
Kadosh	Holly - Saintly
Kamatz	Vowel
Katnut	Smallness
Kav	Ray - Line
Keli	Recipient -Vessel
Kelim	Recipients - Vessels

Keter	Sephira - Crown
Keter, Hokhma, Bina (KHB)	Keter, Hokhma, Bina (KHB)
KHB	Keter, Ho'hma and Binah
Kilkul	Corruption - Deterioration
Kipul Reglaim	Folding of the legs
Klipa	Husk (negative force)
Leida	Birth
Lekabel	To receive
Levush	Garment
Levushim	Garments
Ma'akeh	Parapet (railing)
Maggid	Celestial mentor
MaH	Miluy (spelling) of the name YKVK with a total of 45
Makif	Encircling light
Makifin	Encircling lights
Makom	Place, space. One of the names of G-d
Malbush	Clothe
Malbushim	Clothes
Malkin	Kings of Edom – corresponding to Z'aT
Mayim Dukhrin	Masculine waters
Mayim Nukvin	Feminine waters
M"D	Mayim Dukhrin (masculine waters)
Medaber	Speaking
Melakhim	Kings

Melekh	King
Metsa'h	Forhead
Mida	Attribute -Qualitie - Measure
Midat ha Din	The attribute of Judgment
Midat ha Rakhamim	The attribute of Mercy
Miluy	Letters that are added for the spelling of each individual letter
Mitsva	Commandment
Mitsvot	Commandments
M''N (MaN)	Mayim Nukvin (feminine waters)
MNTSP''KH	Five Gevurot
Moa'h	Brain
Mo'ha Stimaa	One of three heads of Arikh Anpin (Hokhma)
Mo'hin	Brains
Mo'hin of Gadlut	Brains of growth
Mo'hin of Katnut	Brains of infancy
Nefashot	Souls
Nefesh	Soul - First level of the soul
NRN	Nefesh, Ruach, Neshama
Nefilah	Fall
Nekevah	Female - Feminine
Nekudim	Punctuation - Vowels
Neshama	Soul - Third level of the soul
Neshamot	Souls
Neshikin	Kiss
Nessirah	Cutting - separation
Netsah	Sephira -splendor

NHY	Netsah, Hod and Yesod
Nikud	Punctuation
Nitsut	Spark
Nitsutsot	Sparks
NRNHY	Nefesh, Ruah, Neshama, Hayah and Yehidah
Nukvah	The Feminine. Sephira Malhut – Rahel, Leah
'Olam	World
'Olam Ha'Akudim	The world of the attached
'Olam HaNikoudim	The world of points
'Olamot	Worlds
Or	Light
Or Penimi	Inner Light
Or Yashar	Straight light
Panim	Face or Front
Panim B A'hor	Face to back
Panin B Panim	Face to Face
Partsuf	Visage - countenance. Configuration of one or more Sephirot acting in coordination.
Partsufim	Plural of Partsuf
Peah	Edge
Pnimi	Inner - Internal
Pnimiut	Internality
Raglayim	Legs
Ragle Arikh Anpin	Legs of Arikh Anpin
Ra'hamim	Mercy
Ra'hel	Partsuf Nukvah

Rapa'h	288 (numeric value)
Rapa'h Nitsutsot	288 sparks
Ratson	Desire - Will
Reisha	Head
Reshimu	Imprint - trace
Reshit	Beginning - First
Rosh	Head
Rua'h	Soul - Second level of the soul
Ru'hani	Spiritual
Ru'haniut	Spirituality
SaG	Miluy (spelling) of the name YKVK with a total of 63
Seder	Order
Sephira	Light, quality or attribute contained in a keli.
Sephirot	Plural of Sephira
Sha'ar	Gate - Portal
Shabbetai Tsevi	Fake Messiah who converted to Islam
Shalem	Complete
Shekhina	Divine presence
Shvira	Breaking
Shvirat Hakelim	Breaking of the vessels
Sitra A'hra	Negative force
S"M	Name of the destructive Angel
Sod	Secret
Ta'amim	Cantillation notes
Tagin	Crowns on the letters
Telat Rishin	Three Heads

Tevunah 1	Partsuf
Tevunah 2	Partsuf
Tifeeret	Sephira - Beauty
Tikun	Reparation or action
Tikunim	Reparations or actions
Tipah	Drop
Tselem	Shadow - Encircling lights
Tsimtsum	Contraction or retraction
Tsinor	Conduit
Ya'acov	Partsuf
Yashar	Direct - Straight
Ye'hidah	Fifth level of the soul
Yessod	Sephira - Foundation
Yessodot	Plural of Yessod
Yetsirah	World of formation – of the angels
Yi'hud	Unification - Union
Z"A	Partsuf Zeir Anpin
Z"aT	Seven lower Sephirot
Zayin Takhtanot	Seven lower Sephirot
Zeir Anpin	Partsuf Zeir Anpin (Small countenance)
Zivug	Union
Zivugim	Unions
Zohar	The book of splendor, written by Rabbi Shimon Bar Yohai
Z"uN	Zeir Anpin and Nukvah